IRAN'S RESURGENT RESISTANCE

Bipartisan U.S. Delegation Visits with MEK Opposition at Ashraf 3

By Ivan Sascha Sheehan, Ph.D.

IRAN POLICY
COMMITTEE

Copyright © 2020
Iran Policy Committee
Ivan Sascha Sheehan, Ph.D.
1420 N. Charles St.
Baltimore, MD 21201-5779

Printed in the United States of America.
First edition.

ISBN (Hardcover):   978-1-7342292-2-6
ISBN (Paperback):   978-1-7342292-0-2
ISBN (e-book):   978-1-7342292-1-9

Library of Congress Control Number: 2019917878

Library of Congress Cataloging-in-Publication Data

Iran's Resurgent Resistance: Bipartisan U.S. Delegation Visits with MEK Opposition at Ashraf 3

1. Iran. 2. Intelligence. 3. Middle East. 4. Terrorism. 5. History

Photo Credits: All photos credit to NCRI

About the Cover: *Description of Photo.*

This book is dedicated to those
struggling for freedom,
in Iran and around the world...

Former Senior Leaders from the Intelligence Community, Homeland Security, Department of Defense, and Department of State comment on *Iran's Resurgent Resistance*

Louis Freeh, Former Director of the Federal Bureau of Investigation:

Congratulations to Professor Sheehan on his outstanding book, *Iran's Resurgent Resistance*. I was deeply honored to be included in this event. The residents of Ashraf 3 showed me that their inspiration, their prayers, and their commitment to freedom were sufficient to sustain and carry them. Ashraf 3 serves as a testimonial to what can be achieved throughout Iran if a progressive government replaces the existing fundamentalist regime.

Iran's Resurgent Resistance well documents the Martyrs Exhibition. This is more than an exhibition. It is an evidence room with photographs and digital records. It is time to put all of the documentation together like the Simon Wiesenthal Center did after World War II. The Martyrs Exhibition is a catalyst for criminal accountability, just as Ashraf 3 is the starting point for a democratic Iran.

Governor Tom Ridge, First Secretary of Homeland Security:

"You can imprison a man or a woman, but you cannot kill an idea." Like Professor Sheehan, I met several people at Ashraf 3 who had been imprisoned and tortured. Each of them, and those who did not survive, are human tributes to courage and sacrifice. Iranians have a great culture and history that are rich in both tradition and contributions to the rest of the world, but they are not well represented by the regime in Tehran.

Sometimes in our lives we have the opportunity to pursue and embrace causes bigger than ourselves. The residents of Ashraf 3 have dedicated their lives to an open, pluralistic, non-nuclear, and democratic Iran. As thoroughly documented in *Iran's Resurgent Resistance*, the relentless pursuit of justice and liberty by the residents of Ashraf 3 continues to this day. In the end, they will prevail.

General (Ret.) James T. Conway, 34th Commandant of the U.S. Marine Corps:

Thank you to Professor Sheehan for putting into writing what I personally witnessed at Ashraf 3. The residents of Ashraf 3 were not the first to show me the ability to endure loss and yet move on through courage and determination; I have witnessed these traits time and again within the United States Marine Corps. However, within the MEK, I once again saw the sense of unit cohesion, loyalty and dedication to each other. Another commonality that the residents of Ashraf 3 have with U.S. Marines is their ability to "improvise, adapt, and overcome."

In *Iran's Resurgent Resistance*, Professor Sheehan notes the strong bond between the residents and the American military officers who worked with the MEK in Iraq. These bonds are among the greatest testimonials to the MEK that can be made.

Marc Ginsberg, Former U.S. Ambassador to Morocco and White House Middle East Adviser.

On the portraits of each of our aspirations, there's a field of dreams and hopes. There are successes and there are failures. There are achievements as well as setbacks. But the one thing that drives us Americans is the belief that what we wish to achieve for ourselves can be achieved by all people who aspire to freedom, liberty, and dignity. This field of dreams is shared by everyone who was present at the gathering of the Iranian opposition in Albania during summer 2019. The aspirations we have for the people of Ashraf 3 and the people of Iran are that they achieve the support and the dignity they so rightfully deserve. To each of the residents of Ashraf 3 please know Shoma Behtarini (you are the best). Thank you to Professor Sheehan for documenting for the world what we all witnessed during the U.S. delegation's visit with the Iranian opposition.

TABLE OF CONTENTS

Preface

During the summer of 2019, my wife Hadassah and I walked through the Exhibition Hall at Ashraf 3 in Albania with Mrs. Maryam Rajavi, the leader of the National Council of Resistance of Iran (NCRI). We saw the moving tributes to the more than 120,000 Iranians killed by their own government. We heard terrible stories from people who were imprisoned and tortured. We learned of families torn apart, lives upended, and enormous human potential squandered.

It was particularly emotional for Hadassah, whose parents survived the Holocaust while most of their family members were murdered by the Nazis. We were deeply saddened by what we saw in that Exhibition Hall, but still left Ashraf 3 with hope. Our hope was inspired first by the resilience of the residents there — particularly the younger men and women who are so devoted to the cause of freedom and confident that Iran's future will be better than its present — and second because of the continuing protests to the Iranian regime in cities and towns throughout Iran.

It is time for the government of Iran to be held accountable and the people of Iran to be freed. The NCRI is a coalition of Iranian freedom fighting organizations, including the Mujahedin-e Khalq (MEK). It is the largest and most effective of the organizations opposing the current regime. It has many members in exile outside of Iran and many members working for freedom inside Iran.

This book, *Iran's Resurgent Resistance*, is about the visit of so many from around the world to Ashraf 3 last summer. I hope it will be read by policymakers inside the U.S. and that it will be a source of great encouragement to all who care about the cause of freedom throughout the world.

Joseph I. Lieberman
November 2019

Foreword

Senator Robert Torricelli and Ambassador Robert Joseph

For forty years, the regime in Iran has worked relentlessly to annihilate its strongest and most influential opponent, the Mujahedin-e Khalq (MEK). It has executed tens of thousands of MEK followers inside Iran in what is increasingly recognized as a crime against humanity. And it has sought to neutralize all MEK support outside Iran, employing every political and propaganda tool that it controls.

But why? How did Iran's theocratic rulers come to be so fixated on a long-exiled opposition group and what does this mean for U.S. policy toward Iran?

A visit by a bipartisan delegation of senior former U.S. officials to Ashraf 3, the MEK's new home in Albania, provided an opportunity to search for answers to these questions. Our fact-finding expedition gained firsthand insights that led us to conclude what scholars have long understood but policymakers have been reluctant to acknowledge: Iran fears its own people more than it does regional or global powers.

The MEK's presence at the center of the National Council of Resistance of Iran (NCRI), the opposition's Paris-based parliament-in-exile, makes the NCRI a viable and formidable alternative to the mullahs' tyranny. The very existence of this alternative, and its platform of a free, democratic and secular Iran, represents an existential threat to the corrupt clerical dictatorship that controls the people of Iran through fear and brutality.

The argument that there is no popular or credible alternative to theocratic rule has sustained the regime's rulers for too long. The MEK is well-organized, has capable leadership, espouses democratic values, has an impressive track record of resistance, and enjoys considerable support within Iran and among the diaspora. That the group is capable of coalescing domestic support while garnering international recognition means that it must be part of any effective policy toward Tehran.

Decades of false allegations against the MEK, many advanced by Iranian intelligence services, are aimed at convincing U.S. policy makers and influencers that the regime's despotism is an immovable fixture of the Middle East landscape. This falsehood has worked to limit policy options available to U.S. policymakers and curtailed the effectiveness of the country's most credible change agents: the voiceless Iranian people and their organized resistance.

But our five days at Ashraf 3 dealt a crushing blow to these disinformation efforts and influence operations. *Iran's Resurgent Resistance* chronicles our delegation's observations and shared experiences during which we had virtually unrestricted access to every corner of MEK's facilities, as well as its members and leadership. We toured exhibits along with more than 350 prominent dignitaries from 47 countries, participated in seminars, conducted interviews, and fielded questions from the media.

Most of all, we listened, and we learned from the residents. Though nearly 900 residents of the new facility had endured torture in prisons under the Shah's dictatorship or the ayatollahs' rule, we met determined men and women who were eager to topple the regime and establish freedom in their homeland. Their optimism was infectious, their courage inspiring.

Professor Sheehan's authoritative account of what we witnessed lays bare the regime's longstanding anti-MEK campaign and provides an eyewitness look at the group's leadership, rank-and-file, organizational structure, and potential as a viable alternative to clerical rule.

What we saw at Ashraf 3 was a look into Iran's democratic future. This book tells the story of those who are ready to lead the charge for change and give voice to the Iranian people's aspirations for freedom.

Introduction

For four decades, Western policy toward Iran has been anchored in a conceptual scheme that has relied on inaccurate assessments, not only of the ruling regime in Tehran but also of the broader sociopolitical dynamics in the country. Even today, as Tehran-inspired fires sweep through the region and international maritime security in the Gulf is compromised, familiar voices advance dubious arguments that have long motivated a troubled Iran policy. U.S. officials in particular have routinely failed to demonstrate an accurate understanding of the regime's nature, temperament, designs, and dispositions. Common among these failures is a nearly complete dismissal of a critical element needed to bring lasting change to the country: the Iranian people.

The conviction that there is no popular alternative to the current regime in Tehran sustains the false notion that Western powers have no option but to deal with the regime's theocratic rulers. Not surprisingly, the main promoter and principal beneficiary of this argument has been the Iranian regime itself. Equally troubling is that this same logic has fueled unnecessarily partisan wars in Washington at a time when common sense dictates that bipartisan U.S. officials should be united in opposition to Iran's dictatorship and in support of the Iranian people's aspirations for a democratic future. To chart a new course for Iran policy, the U.S. must therefore convince key allies to line up behind a new vision for Iran — one ideally characterized by a free, democratic, and pro-Western society that rejects authoritarian rule, whether illustrated by the rule of the deposed Shah in 1979 or the ayatollahs today.

Against this backdrop, it is not surprising that Tehran has conducted a relentless, decades-long barrage of smears to demonize popular opponents like the People's Mojahedin Organization of Iran (PMOI), also known by its Farsi name, the Mujahedin-e Khalq (MEK). The PMOI/MEK has been the principal opposition to clerical rule since the immediate aftermath of the 1979 Revolution, and the group has only grown in strength, popularity, and prowess since. The regime's rulers routinely refer to their well-organized foe as a "terrorist organization" or "cult," and tag it derisively with pejorative labels designed to cut off conversation and diminish its standing. Regrettably, this strategy has proven effective. Who after all wishes to associate with "terrorists" or "cults" or is willing to cast their lot with an organization reduced to a mere caricature of its core commitments?

Tehran's efforts — underhanded as they are — have also been tactically savvy. Disarmed of a de-facto strategic alliance with the Iranian people, and operating in a space where the regime is an immovable fixture of the Middle East landscape, U.S. officials have naively sought to engage Iran's hostile rulers in the hopes of striking deals in the interest of peace and security, such as the deeply flawed Joint Comprehensive Plan of Action with Iran (JCPOA).

A more strategic approach, however, involves dealing with foundational issues that have long haunted bilateral relations, including Tehran's regional designs, support of terrorism, nuclear proliferation, and myriad human rights violations. These fundamental issues could be tackled head on by upholding the Iranian people's aspirations for a more liberal future. Moreover, they could prompt a critical examination of key issues that challenge the very raison d'être of the regime.

Questions therefore arise: Why has there been such historical reluctance on the part of U.S. officials to engage Iran's principal opposition movement? How well does Washington really know Tehran? Have U.S. officials fallen victim to the regime's propaganda? And, how true is it that there is no alternative to Iran's despotic leaders?

In the pages that follow, I share personal reflections from a recent journey deep into Iran's resistance community. My visit with Iran's freedom fighters — alongside a bipartisan delegation of senior

U.S. officials — reveals how Iran's principal opposition to clerical rule has been falsely portrayed in Washington and intentionally besmirched.

One can be shocked but hardly surprised by such a realization. Since inception, the Iranian regime has feared internal threats more than external pressure and few organizations pose a more lethal threat to the regime's existence than the MEK. In a Machiavellian sense, the regime's rulers are to be credited with the comprehensive, if unscrupulous, manner with which they have addressed their homegrown but exiled challengers. For decades, Iran's rulers have bought influence in the academic community, at prominent think tanks, and by compromising journalists and media outlets to engage in a massive and coordinated influence operation. This has allowed the regime to spread disinformation and propaganda with impunity — at least until now.

In this book, I challenge the false narratives peddled by Tehran's illiberal apologists, examine the opposition's call for a democratic future, and outline the implications for a more effective U.S. policy toward Iran.

The Alternative

In July 2019, a bipartisan delegation made up of senior U.S. officials and prominent individuals visited thousands of courageous Iranian democracy activists living in exile in Albania, home to "Ashraf 3," where the strongest, best organized, and most influential Iranian opposition movement, the MEK, has built an impressive base. Joining us in Tirana were more than 350 prominent dignitaries from 47 countries.

What we witnessed was eye-opening and deeply promising: A cohesive political opposition movement, with a long history of struggle against fundamentalism and dictatorship, guided by

What we witnessed was eye-opening and deeply promising: A cohesive political opposition movement, with a long history of struggle against fundamentalism and dictatorship, guided by gifted female leadership, with a well-defined political platform, and an intricate network of passionate supporters inside Iran and across the world, eager to topple the regime in Tehran from within. It was like looking into Iran's democratic future.

gifted female leadership, with a well-defined political platform, and an intricate network of passionate supporters inside Iran and across the world, eager to topple the regime in Tehran from within. It was like looking into Iran's democratic future.

Our U.S. delegation included four-star generals, Democrats, Republicans, independents, liberals, conservatives, foreign policy experts, sitting members of Congress, former cabinet members, ambassadors, intelligence experts, military officers, governors, academics, and noted human rights advocates. While in Albania, we encountered evidence of both horrific acts of tyranny and heroic acts of resistance. These findings constitute an authoritative body of evidence and opinions that are regrettably too often excluded from the parochial mainstream view of Iranian politics in Washington.

To be clear, American policy to date has been reliably critical of Tehran but generally placatory when it counts the most. Though the plight of the Iranian people and their brutal dictators has been given episodic attention, it has been largely ignored at defining moments.

Confident of the West's conciliatory attitude that, at times, has even morphed into naked appeasement, Tehran regularly amplifies domestic suppression to curtail dissent and promulgates instability abroad. With the regime facing fierce contemporary protests at home, there is increasing recognition that a consistent focus on the Iranian people's democratic plight could change the calculus altogether by presenting the regime's rulers with an existential crisis. Iranian officials, including Supreme Leader Ali Khamenei and President Hassan Rouhani, have publicly described the MEK as the leading voice of anti-regime protests since at least 2018, and the opposition has the regime running scared.

About Ashraf 3

The main entrance to Ashraf 3, the MEK's new residence near Tirana, Albania. Hundreds of residents are lined up to greet more than 350 foreign dignitaries from 47 countries during five days of events celebrating Ashraf 3's inauguration in July 2019.

The MEK invited dignitaries from around the world in July 2019, upon completion of its newly built home, by organizing an international conference and providing access to every corner of its facilities, as well as to its members and leadership. Until this time, the MEK were housed in Iraq, where insecurity and instability made it all but impossible for international visitors to meet with the organization's primary cadre of activists. The Iranian regime and its proxies in Iraq prevented any access by outside observers to Ashraf and a Congressional delegation which traveled to Iraq in June 2011, were denied access to MEK facility by then Prime Minister Nouri al-Maliki, a close ally of Iran, as

An aerial photo of Ashraf 3 undergoing construction in 2018. Ashraf 3 was inaugurated in July 2019.

20

revealed by senior subcommittee chairs of the House Foreign Affairs Committee. Not only the Iraqi Government prevented access to MEK facilities, but conducted attacks on the residents repeatedly from 2009 to 2013, where over 140 MEK members were killed. As a result, the Iranian regime's propaganda machine and its apologists in the West scored success by circulating rumors and disinformation about the group.

Located on a magnificent mountainous landscape in Albania, the MEK's sprawling compound — known as "Ashraf 3" — was named after two former camps with the same name in Iraq. The MEK was founded in 1965 by a group of university graduates with deeply rooted beliefs in nationalism, democracy, and independence. They were inspired by leaders of the Constitutional Revolution, Sattar Khan and Bagher Khan,[1] and nationalist icons like Dr. Mohammad Mossadeq. Since this time, the organization has grown into a full-fledged political powerhouse that even its adversaries describe

1 The Ayatollahs and the MEK: Iran's Crumbling Influence Operation, University of Baltimore College of Public Affairs, June 24, 2019. <https://www.amazon.com/Ayatollahs-MEK-Crumbling-Influence-Operation/dp/0578536099>

as the best organized and most formidable opposition to the contemporary Iranian theocracy.

The organization displays democratic attributes that have only deepened during its 54-year history. As but one illustration of this, the entire Central Council is currently led by women, a major shift that started in the 1980s. Moreover, among the approximately 2,500 residents of Ashraf 3, roughly 1,000 are women — many of them former political prisoners who were brutally tortured by the misogynistic regime in Tehran.

Situated between the Albanian capital of Tirana to the east and the Adriatic Sea to the west, Ashraf 3 sits atop a series of former farmlands. A relatively large enclave now housing over 2,500 MEK activists, the "city" boasts residential quarters, dozens of facilities, shopping centers, libraries, medical clinics, pharmacies, dining halls, museums, large auditoriums, fitness centers, soccer fields, pools, and even a concert hall.

21

Astonishingly, there was no infrastructure, running water, or electricity in this area as recently as 2018 when the residents first arrived. The residents built the city in less than 20 months, a feat of construction and engineering magic that speaks to the MEK's intellectual and organizational prowess. It is worth noting that this is the third time they have built a city during their decades in exile, but the latest one in Albania is, by any measure, extraordinarily impressive.

From 1986 onwards, many of the residents built and resided in "Ashraf 1" in Iraq's Diyala Province, near the Iran-Iraq border. In the 1980s the MEK maintained what amounted to a liberation army and were equipped with tanks and armored vehicles. After the 2003 invasion of Iraq by U.S.-led multinational forces, however, the MEK voluntarily disarmed its significant cache of weapons. Defenseless and unarmed, its members were persecuted by successive Iraqi governments eager to curry favor with the Iranian mullahs, who consider the MEK their archenemies. In fact, the regime asked for the MEK's total annihilation or complete surrender. A period of severe persecution and suffering ensued for the MEK in Iraq, lasting approximately 14 years.

Beginning in 2009, an impressive list of prominent intellectuals, former officials, and personalities spoke on behalf of the MEK's safety and protection by U.S. forces in Iraq. Senior Members of Congress in both chambers in a bi-partisan way were defending MEK's safety and security and had introduced resolutions with a majority co-sponsors, as well as languages in authorization bills including the Defense Authorization Bill which was signed into law, all in support of the well being of these dissidents. Yet scores of opposition members were killed in multiple terrorist and rocket attacks conducted by the Iranian regime and its Iraqi allies and proxies. In 2016, all of the MEK activists were safely relocated from Iraq to Tirana, the Albanian capital. The fact that they safely relocated to Europe with their organizational structure and leadership still intact marked a remarkable success for the resistance and, in equal measure, a humiliating defeat for Tehran.

Our Experience at Ashraf 3

In summer 2019, I, along with international dignitaries from around the world, had a rare opportunity to meet with MEK members face-to-face. During our visit, I spoke to the residents individually. I found them to be highly educated, well spoken (many of them native English speakers), articulate, cultured, civilized, and genuinely interested in a democratic future. A large number had lost family members in gruesome massacres and human rights tragedies perpetrated by the regime. Many also had family members in Iran, who continue to be arrested and persecuted by the regime for their association with the MEK to this day.

Current and former world leaders from four continents pose for a photo with Mrs. Maryam Rajavi, the President-elect of the National Council of Resistance of Iran, to memorialize the July 2019 inauguration of Ashraf 3, the MEK's new residence in Albania.

> U.S. officials visiting Ashraf 3 in summer 2019 learned that the MEK is highly professional, well organized, dedicated to an unending struggle against the regime, and extremely knowledgeable about Iran's history and contemporary politics — including the internal dynamics of the regime itself.

24

U.S. officials visiting Ashraf 3 in summer 2019 learned that the MEK is highly professional, well organized, dedicated to an unending struggle against the regime, and extremely knowledgeable about Iran's history and contemporary politics — including the internal dynamics of the regime itself. In fact, they were the first to expose the regime's nuclear weapons program in Natanz and Arak in August 2002, triggering an international monitoring program and global condemnation of the regime.

I was impressed by the ingenuity of the Ashraf 3's architects and builders who managed to chronicle their historic journey. Indeed, the facility was built with jaw-dropping speed, after just more than a year of construction frenzy. The structures and monuments at Ashraf 3 take their cue from icons of freedom and sacrifice across the world, especially the French and the Americans. The entrance to Ashraf 3, for example, resembles striking scenes from Versailles. The road leading to the gate is flanked with dozens of tall flagpoles hoisting the national banners of many countries across the globe. The "Lion and Sun" insignia of modern Iran is prominently displayed, in contrast to the religiously inspired insignia of the Iranian regime's current flag.

*The **Taq-e Nosrat**, or Iran's version of the Arc de Triomphe in Paris, is a symbolic replica of the famous entrance to Iran's national parliament, built following the Constitutional Revolution of 1906, an emblematic nod to a defining feature of the MEK's historical identity.*

Past the lion statues that flank both sides of the large entrance gate, I saw a towering "Taq-e Nosrat," or Iran's version of the Arc de Triomphe in Paris (and almost as tall). In the middle of the pearly granite monument, a huge Iranian national flag waved in the summer breeze, mimicking the French version. Symbolically, the "Taq" is a replica of the famous entrance to Iran's national parliament built in 1906. It is an emblematic nod to a defining feature of the MEK's historical identity, which spans back a century to the Constitutional Revolution of 1906 when

The Memorial Wall in Ashraf 3 pays homage to the tens of thousands of MEK members and other martyrs fallen for the cause of Iran's freedom. It resembles the design of the World War II Memorial in Washington, D.C. The memorial features a water and fire structure that represents "The Eternal Flame of Freedom."

the Iranian people rose up against the monarchy to demand a democratically elected national parliament. Those dreams were dashed by the dictators of the Pahlavi dynasty starting in the 1920s.

Ashraf 3 has several other large and elaborate monuments, the most prominent of which pays homage to the tens of thousands of martyrs and MEK members fallen for the cause of Iran's freedom. The "Memorial Wall" resembles the design of the World War II Memorial in Washington, D.C., commemorating the memory of those fallen in the war against Hitler's fascism. The MEK is adamant that it is actively engaged in a noble and historic struggle against the "religious fascism" of the mullahs ruling Iran.

The Ashraf 3 memorial includes 18 granite pillars, each about 15 feet tall, forming a semicircle, with a large 40-foot tall triumphal arch in the middle. Each pillar has been inscribed with the names of dozens of MEK activists who have "fallen for freedom." In the middle is a water feature with a central fire that represents "the eternal flame of freedom." Visitors to Washington, D.C.'s memorial

The "Memorial Wall" resembles the design of the World War II Memorial in Washington, D.C. The MEK is adamant that it is actively engaged in a noble and historic struggle against the "religious fascism" of the mullahs ruling Iran.

can relate since the Freedom Wall has a similar message: "Here we mark the price of freedom." The MEK has particularly strong reverence for the Iranian people's sacrifices, which it says total more than 120,000 killed by the regime.

The Exhibition Hall near the memorial captures pictures and stories dedicated to "120 Years of the Iranian People's Struggle for Freedom" (since around the time of the 1906 Constitutional Revolution). On the outside wall of the hall, one sees huge portraits of Iran's revolutionary leaders from 1906, to the nationalist movement of the 1950s, to the anti-monarchical democratic movement of the 1960s and 1970s, to the anti-clerical regime movement of the 1980s, 1990s and 2000s. Two of the figures are from the Constitutional Revolution era, two from the oil nationalization movement of the 1950s (overthrown by a U.S. and British-sponsored coup d'état), one is an MEK founder, two are slain leaders of the MEK, and the last is Massoud Rajavi, the historical leader of the Resistance. Again, the aim of these landmarks and images is to insist and convey the MEK's historical lineage and political identity. Some in the West continue to fall victim to the regime's misleading propaganda designed to demonize and dismiss the movement as a fringe element with a suspect historical identity and very little social support inside Iran.

This false narrative is challenged when one witnesses, as I did, the movement's extraordinary history of sacrifice, anguish,

The Ashraf 3 memorial includes 18 granite pillars, each about 15 feet tall, inscribed with the names of dozens of MEK activists who have "fallen for freedom" in what the MEK insists is a noble and historic struggle against the "religious fascism" of the mullahs ruling Iran.

and loss. Within the Exhibition Hall, which many of us found particularly poignant, there were photographs and stories of the Iranian regime's grotesque human rights violations. Pictures of girls, as young as 13, killed by the regime for reading MEK newspapers are plastered over huge walls. Works of art made by political prisoners while in captivity, thousands of whom were later massacred in 1988, are especially effective reminders that convey the inspiring human stories that lie behind many of the regime's gruesome crimes. According to one American visitor, "We saw the darkness, the numbers of destruction, and I heard the voices of those who shared their stories from prison, from losing members of their family, their communities, and I saw the light in their eyes."

The Exhibition Hall displayed depictions of the tens of thousands of executed people, brave family survivors, the next generations, and especially the courageous women that were not deterred by the misogynist mullahs' reign of terror. In fact, the title "exhibition"

In the Exhibition Hall, photographs and stories depict the Iranian regime's grotesque human rights violations. Pictures of girls as young as 13, killed by the regime for reading MEK newspapers, are plastered over huge walls.

hardly does what I saw justice. As one senior former U.S. official put it, the room actually constituted an evidence chamber complete with photographs, details and digital records. There were also eyewitnesses and former political prisoners on hand to convey the frightful circumstances they faced and the courageous paths they walked. I came to believe that it essential to have this evidence hall maintained for future visitors, if only to aid in bringing the regime's human rights violators to account for their many crimes.

Still, the exhibition was not only about the regime's abuses. It was also a powerful reminder of the MEK's vast and extensive presence within the country. The hall had sections on each of Iran's 31 provinces, demonstrating how the victims, MEK members and sympathizers, hailed from almost every city and province of the Iranian nation. It demonstrated that the MEK has broad social backing, with many of the tens of thousands of victims having come from a social milieu that to this day

The handiwork of political prisoner Batool Abdi, a member of the MEK. She made this during her incarceration in the 1980s. Batool was later executed.

30

condemns the regime's heinous crimes against members and supporters of the organization. Many of these surviving former friends, relatives, classmates, neighbors and work colleagues in Iran continue to provide moral and financial support to the MEK in memory of the heroes killed in their small towns and communities.

The slain martyrs in more than 31 provinces and hundreds of cities, towns and villages attest to a broad social network made up of former neighbors, acquaintances, family members, relatives, and colleagues, who now form the MEK's backbone. They provide the organization with vital financial, moral, intelligence, and social support.

The Exhibition Hall has sections on each of Iran's 31 provinces, showing how the victims, MEK members, hailed from almost every city and province. It is a powerful reminder of the MEK's extensive presence. These pictures display the provinces of Isfahan, Charmahal Bakhtiari, Sistan & Baluchistan (top), and Hormozgan (bottom).

The experience emanating from the MEK's construction of Ashraf 3 is yet another indication of what forward-thinking people can achieve. Built in less than 20 months, the city now has dozens of facilities and amenities, and it reflects well the capabilities of Iran's organized opposition.

Some of the names and pictures of the MEK members and sympathizers from provinces of Yazd and Kerman in the south (top), Semnan and Golestan in the north (bottom), who were executed by the clerical regime.

In fact, Ashraf 3 stands as a testament to the fact that this movement presents a viable alternative to the regime and that Iran is neither Syria nor Libya. The existence of a viable alternative — one that erects shining cities wherever they are deposited, from Iraq to Albania — should be considered by U.S.

Jean-Francois Legaret, Mayor of Paris' 1st District presented a plaque to Ms. Zohreh Akhyani, the MEK's Secretary General (2011-2017), declaring Paris' 1st district as a sister city of Ashraf 3.

33

officials hoping to examine who best can replace the theocratic regime, restore order after decades of unrest, and bring about a peaceful transition of power.

Even more important than the impressive buildings and memorials that the residents have built, however, is the spirit of Ashraf

The existence of a viable alternative – one that erects shining cities wherever they are deposited, from Iraq to Albania – should be considered by U.S. officials hoping to examine who best can replace the theocratic regime, restore order after decades of unrest, and bring about a peaceful transition of power.

3. Many in our U.S. delegation and other international visitors too could not help but be filled with optimism for Iran's future. Indeed, Ashraf 3 embodies a symbol of hope for a brighter future but also sends a clear message to Tehran's rulers. The residents

The two Olympic-size indoor swimming pools are particularly useful for those residents who suffered injuries as a result of either years of incarceration in the clerical regime's prisons, or during violent assaults launched by the Iraqi government acting at Iran's behest during the 7-year siege of the MEK's bases in Iraq.

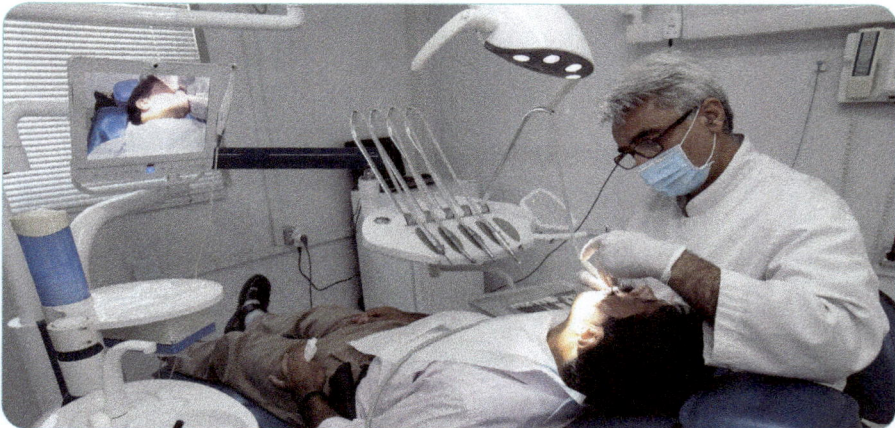

The dental clinic is operated by MEK doctors and specialists. All of the movement's medical equipment and facilities were either destroyed or confiscated by the Iraqi regime during the 2009—2016 siege of Ashraf 1 & 2. The medical clinic at Ashraf 3, like all other facilities, was built and equipped by the MEK and financed by their vast support network among the Iranian diaspora.

could have just as well inscribed on the entrance gate: "After murdering tens of thousands of our people, family members and friends, after five intelligence teams attempted to murder and bomb the MEK in Europe and the U.S. in just the past few

A man-made creek flows through Ashraf 3, beautifully designed and landscaped. In a hint to the Iran of the future envisioned by the group, aesthetics have been given attention equal to that of the demands of convenience and functionality.

*The entrance to **Park-e Meli**, a beautiful park where the always-busy residents can relax and unwind.*

years, and after all of the terrorist attacks in Iraq, you failed. The women and men of the resistance have survived, and they are stronger than ever. There is still an alternative. And the world is now coming to support it."

The state-of-the-art, fully equipped gymnasium is very popular with the MEK members at Ashraf 3. Similar to the swimming pools, residents working to overcome past injuries use the facility for supervised physical rehabilitation and therapy.

Chelcheragh *is the supermarket, operated and stocked by MEK staff, serving the residents' needs.*

Five Days with Iran's Opposition

The July 2019 international conference at Ashraf 3 lasted for five days. Most of the U.S. delegation attended the events at the MEK's headquarters for the full duration of the conference, which included topics such as the 1988 massacre, international policy toward Iran, women's role in Iranian politics, and the role of the Iranian regime in the Arab World.

For 15 years prior to this, Iran's parliament-in-exile, the National Council of Resistance of Iran (NCRI), a broad democratic coalition that has the MEK as its principal organization, held large international gatherings near Paris to call for a free and democratic Iran. These massive events drew tens of thousands of Iranians who were joined by hundreds of prominent dignitaries, former ministers, heads of state, politicians, parliamentarians, and foreign policy experts from around the world who embraced regime change by the Iranian people and the Iranian Resistance. Many of the attendees carried messages of support endorsed by thousands of other parliamentarians, mayors, human rights activists and Western citizens.

For a number of years, the focus of these gatherings was the protection of members of the MEK who were then residing under brutal conditions in Iraq. Dozens of MEK members in Iraq were killed during indiscriminate terrorist attacks conducted or inspired by the Iranian regime and its proxies in Baghdad.

This year, however, the Free Iran Gathering convened at what many described as the heart of Iranian resistance, in the newly established Ashraf 3 in Albania, with members of the MEK themselves, all of whom were safely relocated to Albania in 2016. It was an emotional reunion with thousands of people who had been calling for the MEK's protection for more than a decade. Internationally, thousands of Iranian exiles held solidarity protests in Brussels (June 15), Washington D.C. (June 21), Berlin (July 6), Stockholm (July 20), and London (July 27).

The Albanian delegation was presented by Pandeli Majko, the State Minister for Diaspora, Former Prime Minister of Albania, as well as parliamentarians and officials of political parties.

From left, General James Conway, former Albanian President and Prime Minister Sali Berisha, former Albanian Defense Minister, Fatmir Mediu, and General George Casey talk on the sidelines of the July 13 conference.

38

Starting on July 11, 2019, delegations from 47 nations participated in the Free Iran Gathering at Ashraf 3. These delegations came from all over the world and included high-level representatives from the United States, Canada, the United Kingdom, France, Germany, Italy, Belgium, Australia, Sweden, Norway, Denmark, Algeria, Egypt, Morocco, Saudi Arabia, Jordan, Yemen, Lebanon, Syria (opposition), Bahrain, Turkey, India, and Colombia, and many others. The guests included former heads of state, prime ministers, ministers, party leaders, parliamentarians, cabinet officials, governors, mayors, members of parliaments, senior military commanders and officers (including former U.S. military commanders of Camp Ashraf, Iraq), foreign policy and human rights experts, and women's rights activists. Among them were prominent personalities like President Donald Trump's personal attorney Rudy Giuliani, former Homeland Secretary Tom Ridge, and former Senator Joe Lieberman.

Other delegates visiting Ashraf 3 included former Canadian Prime Minister Stephen Harper, former Canadian Foreign Minister John Baird, former French Foreign and Defense Minister, Michele Alliot-Marie; former French Foreign Minister Bernard Kouchner, former FBI Director Louis Freeh, former Secretary of Homeland Security Tom Ridge, former commandant of the Marine Corps General James Conway, Ambassador Lincoln Bloomfield, Ambassador Robert Joseph, former Senator Robert Torricelli, and former Vice President of the European Parliament Alejo Vidal-Quadras, among many others.

During our visits to Ashraf 3, the American delegation's members had the opportunity to speak personally and privately with dozens

> During our visits to Ashraf 3, the American delegation's members had the opportunity to speak personally and privately with dozens of MEK members, including women, who lead the movement.

Many delegations from Europe attended the large gathering. Mr. Alejo Vidal-Quadras, former Vice President of the European Parliament who headed one of these delegations, is seen speaking at the podium.

40

of MEK members, including women, who lead the movement. For some of us, it was our first time meeting them and hearing their captivating stories of courage, sacrifice and pain firsthand. As was the case with other international dignitaries, we had unfettered access to Ashraf 3, including the community's many facilities and amenities, and unrestricted opportunities to visit with MEK residents. We met with real people with compelling histories and admirable aspirations for the future of Iran and the world.

The audience of several thousand, inspired by Mrs. Rajavi's keynote speech entitled "We will take back Iran," responded jubilantly.

Panel Discussions

The five day "Free Iran" gathering at Ashraf 3 kicked off on Thursday, July 11, with an expert panel discussion entitled "Policy on Iran & a Viable Alternative." Ambassador Lincoln Bloomfield moderated the panel. Among the speakers were Mayor Rudy Giuliani, General James Conway, Ambassador Robert Joseph, Honorable John Baird, Senator Robert Torricelli, and Professor Ivan Sascha Sheehan.

A recurrent theme was that there is a viable democratic alternative to the current regime in Iran, one that is best illustrated by the MEK. Many of the speakers also noted that while the Iranian regime spends enormous time and resources promoting the false

(From right) Professor Ivan Sascha Sheehan (the author), General James Conway, Ambassador Robert Joseph, Mayor Rudy Giuliani, Ambassador Lincoln Bloomfield (moderator), Senator Robert Torricelli, and the Honorable John Baird, address the audience at the panel discussion entitled "Policy on Iran & a Viable Alternative" on July 11, 2019.

> Ashraf 3 and the MEK represent the hope of Iranians for a better future, and a democratic path for Iran that the world community can reasonably support.

narrative that there is no alternative to its rule and that the world has no choice but to deal with it, Ashraf 3 and the MEK represent the hope of Iranians for a better future, and a democratic path for Iran that the world community can reasonably support.

A general consensus at this initial panel discussion was that the Trump administration has made important strides in shifting U.S. policy from the conciliatory gestures of the Obama years to a much firmer stance toward the Islamic Republic of Iran. The April 2019 designation of the IRGC as a Foreign Terrorist Organization (FTO), for example, was an illustration of President Trump's willingness to confront the Islamic Republic's malign activities in the Middle East and belligerence around the globe.

(From right) Professor Ivan Sascha Sheehan, General James Conway, and Ambassador Robert Joseph at the panel discussion entitled "Policy on Iran & a Viable Alternative" on July 11, 2019.

Nevertheless, there was a collective belief that more could still be done in this regard and that decisive action to strike a significant blow to a regime that has been engaged in repression and the imposition of regional chaos was needed by the White House and the U.S. Congress. U.S. officials in attendance at Ashraf 3 events heard firsthand how bold action by the U.S. serves as a major boost to Iranians seeking to topple the regime from within by giving ordinary Iranians even more reason to take to the streets. In addition to external pressures, it was also agreed that Tehran was feeling the heat from within. The amplification of efforts initiated by Iran's own resistance community over the past two years — particularly those undertaken by the People's Mojahedin Organization of Iran (PMOI/MEK) — have consumed the regime's clerical rulers and prompted a fresh examination of the mullah's hold on power.

Following the panel, members of the American delegation visited the sports facility and even paid a visit to one of the Ashraf 3 bakeries, where the residents were preparing fresh bread as well as pastry.

Hundreds of dignitaries and resident of Ashraf 3 attended the July 11 panel discussion, which was translated simultaneously for the audience into 5 languages by multi-lingual members of the MEK.

Meeting Individual MEK Members

That evening, after attending a three-hour panel on policy options, several members of the American delegation had dinner with dozens of women from the MEK in one of their immaculate dining halls at Ashraf 3. We had an opportunity to speak to them personally and privately. We heard stories of courage, pain, and struggle. They provided incriminating evidence of the regime's crimes against their family members, including executions and torture. Many were young, in their 20s or 30s. Many were multi-lingual and could speak fluent English or French, among other languages. They struck us as highly educated, well-spoken, knowledgeable about global affairs, and genuine in their commitment to a free and democratic Iran, especially for the women in their homeland. They were clearly inspired by their charismatic leader and role model, Mrs. Maryam Rajavi, President-elect of the NCRI for the transition period. Each of us was struck that a viable Muslim movement, led by capable women, with enough courage to stand up to the brutal, misogynistic and extremist regime in the Middle East existed and was prepared to take Iran's clerical rulers to task.

Each of us was struck that a viable Muslim movement, led by capable women, with enough courage to stand up to the brutal, misogynistic and extremist regime in the Middle East existed and was prepared to take Iran's clerical rulers to task.

After the dinner, we continued our conversations with these women. Contrary to the propaganda promulgated by the Iranian regime, there were no "guards" watching over our conversations. We asked difficult questions and we received honest answers — a determination made not only by me but also by senior former U.S. officials with decades of service to the U.S. Intelligence Community. We found these individuals to be intelligent people who could have had any life they wanted in Iran or in the West. Some of them were born in Europe. But they made an informed decision that they had to stand up for a cause larger than themselves. That evening and in the conversations that followed, the Iranian intelligence service's caricature of these extraordinary individuals collapsed all around us.

Other MEK residents we met were similarly sophisticated, motivated, and proud of their historical inheritance and culture. In fact, throughout the meeting we heard extraordinary stories of sacrifice, conviction, separation, and the choice of a lifetime. Residents of Ashraf 3 have dedicated their lives to a cause higher than themselves and are at peace with their decision. They want

46

The American delegation also attended a dinner reception hosted by a group of MEK female members in their immaculate dining hall. As was the case with other international dignitaries, we had unrestricted opportunities to visit with MEK residents.

nothing less than freedom and democracy for their people, rejecting the regime's value system of "power at any price" and instead embracing an unending commitment to "freedom at any cost."

The residents clearly revered nationalist figures like the late Dr. Mohammad Mossaddeq, the first and only democratically elected prime minister whose government was toppled in 1953 by a U.S. and British-led coup. They were also highly educated about topics such as gender equality, pluralism, democracy, and even the American Constitution and U.S. political history. Many were educated in American universities and some even worked in American companies. Not only were they clearly people of free will speaking for themselves with courage and honor, but they did so while bearing witness to the regime's cruelties.

Conference on Struggle for Freedom

On Friday, July 12, international delegations visited the Zohre Hall in Ashraf 3, which was the venue for a conference and exhibition entitled "120 Years of Struggle for Freedom in Iran." The hall boasts a façade depicting Iran's historical heritage at Chehel Sotoun in Isfahan, with the insignia of modern-day Iran. The outside walls of the hall are decorated with large portraits of Iran's contemporary historical figures in the struggle for freedom. They included Sattar Khan, Baqir Khan and Mirza Kuchak Khan, major leaders of the Constitutional Revolution in 1906; Dr. Mohammad Mossadeq, leader of Iran's nationalist movement, along with his foreign minister, Dr. Hossein Fatemi, who was executed by the Shah's regime;

At the Exhibition Hall, a conference was attended by hundreds of political and human rights personalities, as well as members of the press, where they heard stories of the victims of repression in Iran.

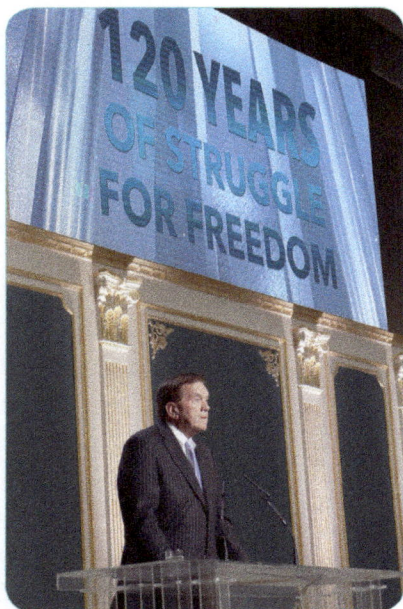

First Secretary of Homeland Security the Honorable Tom Ridge, addresses the conference and exhibition entitled "120 Years of Struggle for Freedom in Iran.

50

Mohammad Hanifnejad, one of the MEK's founders; Ashraf Rajavi and Moussa Khiabani, two post-revolutionary leaders of the MEK killed in 1982; and finally, Massoud Rajavi, the historical leader of the Iranian Resistance.

The exhibition hall hosted a tribute to the 120-year struggle for freedom, and particularly the resistance of the Iranian people against the mullahs. The organizers convened a conference there on Friday, July 12, 2019, which was attended by hundreds of political and human rights personalities, as well as

International delegations joined the American delegation at the July 12 event, attended by hundreds of political and human rights leaders, as well as members of the press.

These Ashraf 3 residents shared the horrific ordeals they personally experienced inside Iran regime's dungeons.

members of the press. Several of the guest dignitaries spoke of their admiration for the struggle of the Ashraf residents and the Iranian people's aspirations for freedom.

Various delegations from Ashraf residents made presentations on subjects ranging from the uprising in Iran and the role of the MEK, the Iranian regime's terrorism, the 1988 massacre of political prisoners, continued human rights violations under the current regime, as well as a history of the MEK's years of perseverance in camps Ashraf and Liberty in Iraq from 2003 to 2016.

51

The Ashraf 3 residents' unique perspective on those events that impacted them and their loved ones directly was both informative and touching for the international audience.

After the conference, attendees toured the exhibition hall which chronicles Tehran's human rights violations and learned about the thousands of martyrs for the cause of freedom, some of them teenagers, who had committed no crime but to express a commitment to democracy. Witnesses of torture and imprisonment were present to provide their personal accounts and stories. We witnessed unspeakable evidence that showed acts of torture and murder in Iranian prisons, beginning in the early 1980s. Pictures and stories of executed pregnant women and girls as young as 13 were particularly distressing.

At the same time, these horrific personal stories and accounts revealed the MEK's unyielding commitment to democracy and freedom. Supported by the fact that thousands of their members and sympathizers were executed by the regime, visitors learned that the MEK's political platform for the future of Iran calls for the abolishment of the death penalty. Enough bloodshed, they say. As one guide said to me: "we want to rebuild, not destroy."

Visitors to the exhibition hall learned that more than 120,000 MEK members and supporters died in the cause for freedom in

52

American and international delegations, accompanied by the leader of the Resistance, Mrs. Maryam Rajavi, toured the Exhibition Hall which chronicles Tehran's human rights violations.

Iran, including 30,000 who were massacred in summer 1988 alone. A large section of the exhibition hall was dedicated to this massacre. A row of real size human statues surrounded by barbed wire showed how prisoners were queued up and led to the gallows by the hundreds. Ropes and nooses hanging from the ceiling sought to enhance the experience. It was a chilling reminder of how 30,000 political prisoners were forced to their deaths, even after completing their prison sentences, simply because they refused to condemn the MEK and support the mullahs. This is why, today, the MEK's name is so cherished and revered by survivors. They see it as a continuation and reminder of those slain for their commitment to freedom and democracy in Iran.

In another section of the Exhibition, we saw real size prison cells complete with steel doors and got to experience the eerie atmosphere of the regime's prisons for ourselves. We also saw "cages," rows of 0.5m x 1m spaces separated by small walls, where women prisoners were forced to sit for months without uttering

The exhibition was a chilling reminder of how 30,000 political prisoners were forced to their deaths, even after completing their prison sentences, simply because they refused to condemn the MEK and support the mullahs. This is why, today, the MEK's name is so cherished by survivors.

30,000 political prisoners were forced to their deaths, even after completing their prison sentences, simply because they refused to condemn the MEK and support the mullahs. This is why, today, the MEK's name is so cherished and revered by survivors.

a word. According to eyewitnesses, many became so mentally disturbed they never recovered. We also talked to some of the female survivors.

54

One of the women survivors, Hengameh Haj Hassan, shared her story with me:

In the Exhibition Hall, the delegations saw the replica of "cages," rows of 0.5m x 1m spaces separated by small walls, where women prisoners were forced to sit for months without uttering a word. Female survivors of this torture method were present to describe their ordeal.

"I was a nurse in Tehran. In 1981, I was arrested because I was a MEK supporter. We were taken to the 'cages.' These were small partitions where you could only squat. You couldn't move, you couldn't even cough or sneeze. If we moved, we were tortured. Our eyes were blindfolded. The torturer told us that we would die here. We were only given three minutes per day to go to the bathroom. We couldn't even brush our teeth. The food they gave us was scarce and very dirty. At night, when we were allowed to sleep, they would turn on loudspeakers and play the regime's mourning songs. The torturers sought to break our will and force us to turn our back to our struggle. However, they only made us stronger, as we understood that this proved what we were doing was right."

In 1988, the Iranian regime slaughtered an estimated 30,000 political prisoners, most of them MEK members and sympathizers. Amnesty International has described the 1988 prison massacres as "ongoing crimes against humanity." Indeed, according to Amnesty International:

"Between July and September 1988, the Iranian authorities forcibly disappeared and extrajudicially executed thousands of imprisoned political dissidents in secret and dumped their bodies, mostly in unmarked mass graves. Since then, the authorities have treated the killings as state secrets, tormenting the relatives by refusing to tell them how and why their loved ones were killed and where they are buried. No official has been brought to justice and, in some cases, those involved hold or have held positions of power in Iran. Across the country, the victims were primarily supporters of the PMOI [MEK], both men and women."[2]

---

2 Iran: Blood Soaked Secrets: Why Iran's 1988 prison massacres are ongoing crimes against humanity. Amnesty International, 4 December 2018.

In 1988, the Iranian regime slaughtered an estimated 30,000 political prisoners, most of them MEK members and sympathizers. Amnesty International has described the 1988 prison massacres as "ongoing crimes against humanity."

These two walls in the Exhibition Hall displayed a partial list of the fallen heroes of the MEK from all of Iran's 31 provinces.

At Ashraf 3, Fereshteh Akhlaghi, a female survivor of the regime's torture chambers who has researched the 1988 massacre extensively, said: "This Exhibition is only the tip of the iceberg. In just two years, the regime executed 477 adolescents and youth, including three 12-year-olds. Eight people were 13 years old. 19 individuals were 14 years old. Thirty-two individuals were 15 years old. Others were 16 and 17 years old. 55 pregnant women were executed. One of the pregnant women was summoned by the executioner, who told her he had executed her husband and then offered to release her if she interviewed with state TV. She spat in the judge's face. The regime also executed and tortured the elderly. The mother of the Shafaie family, all of whom were executed, was also executed by the regime. Before her execution, she said, 'I'm proud that I've given my all for freedom.'"

Another female survivor said:

> "The Revolutionary Guards (IRGC) arrested me while I was pregnant. I was taken to Evin prison and the torture chambers. I was transferred to Ward 209. In the cell, I saw four torturers torture my husband in front of me. They also tortured me in front of him. A few days later, they executed him with 75 others. The torturer said, 'I wanted him to never see his son.' The regime executed 50 pregnant women, including Masumeh, the sister of Mrs. Rajavi. The torturers even interrogated the children. They had strapped a small child to a chair in a dark room and tortured her, so she revealed the names of her mother's friends. I managed to escape prison in 1987. One year later, all of those ladies who shared the cell with me were executed in the 1988 massacre."

We heard from another survivor at the time, Mahmoud Royaie, who said:

> "One of my friends was executed five years after his sentence was finished. He was taken to the gallows only because he defended the name of the MEK. Many of the prisoners' families died after their loved ones were executed. The father of one of my friends had a cardiac arrest when he heard about his son's execution. Some of these families are still staring at the pictures of their loved ones and crying after 30 years. Some lost their sanity when their children were executed. The regime even executed the disabled and handicapped."

One of the exhibition hall's areas included a memorial for those who had lost their lives during attacks by the Iranian regime and its proxies on the MEK while they were still in Iraq. The members of the MEK residing at Camps Ashraf and Liberty in Iraq from 2009 to 2016 suffered three ground assaults, five rocket attacks, deprivation of basic life support (such as food, water, and proper sanitation), and denial of reasonable access to timely medical treatment. 168 members lost their lives and 1,487 suffered injuries.

Overall, the exhibition hall demonstrated the MEK's sacrifices and the overwhelming price that its members and sympathizers have paid during 40 years of struggle against religious fascism. In addition, the hall's many maps, names, and images show the MEK's intricate network of support in every neighborhood, town, city, and province of Iran. Indeed, the slain martyrs in more than 31 provinces and hundreds of cities, towns and villages attest to a broad social network made up of former neighbors, acquaintances, family members, relatives, and colleagues, who now form the MEK's backbone. They provide the organization with vital financial, moral, intelligence, and social support.

The Main Event

On Sat July 13, 2019, Ashraf 3 was host to the main event of its five-day global conference: an international gathering of over 350 high-profile dignitaries attending from over 47 countries. Political dignitaries, ministers, prime ministers, diplomats, military figures, human rights activists and parliamentarians lent public support to the MEK's goals of establishing a free, secular and democratic republic in Iran.

Delegates from 47 countries, joined by leaders of the Iranian diaspora overseas and hundreds of Ashraf 3 residents, attended the main event, the July 13 "Free Iran" conference.

According to *The Washington Times* reporting from Ashraf 3, the speed with which the town was built "was enough to make Mr. Giuliani marvel." "This whole city was built in less than two years," Mr. Giuliani said. "If we tried to do this in New York, it would take 15 years and launch 14 corruption investigations."

Several hundred political dignitaries, ministers, prime ministers, diplomats, military figures, human rights activists and parliamentarians lent public support to the MEK's goals of establishing a free, secular and democratic republic in Iran during the July 13 conference.

60

All of the speakers and international delegations expressed strong support for the NCRI's political platform and its President-elect, Mrs. Maryam Rajavi.

Several thousand of Ashraf 3 residents and their guests, cheered as Mrs. Rajavi delivered her keynote speech entitled "We will take back Iran."

Mrs. Rajavi delivered a powerful and emotional call for regime change in Iran in her keynote address, entitled "We will take back Iran."

In her keynote address, entitled "We will take back Iran," Mrs. Rajavi delivered a powerful and emotional call for regime change in Iran. "At the hands of the Mojahedin... through their enormous efforts and hard work, Ashraf 3 was built and now stands tall. But our final destination is Tehran, freed from the occupation of the mullahs," Mrs. Rajavi said.

She expounded on the journey of the Iranian Resistance from resistance to the dictatorship of the mullahs' regime to the prospect of a free and democratic Iran and pointed out the Resistance

> In her keynote address, entitled "We will take back Iran," Mrs. Rajavi delivered a powerful and emotional call for regime change in Iran.

Senator Robert Torricelli introduced the American delegation, which included four-star generals, Democrats, Republicans, independents, liberals, conservatives, foreign policy experts, sitting and former members of Congress, former cabinet members, ambassadors, intelligence experts, military officers, governors, academics, and noted human rights advocates.

movement's unique credentials for bringing about transformative change. Describing the mullahs' 40-year rule as an all-out massacre of human rights, she also called for international accountability.

Mrs. Rajavi emphasized that "the mullahs are counting on inaction and tolerance on the part of the international community. Their calculation is that terrorist operations and warmongering [propagated by the regime] in the region's countries will not cost them very much, at least until the next U.S. presidential election. They say to themselves: 'Let's wait another 16 months and maybe the U.S. will have another president from whom we can extract the same super concessions as we did with the nuclear deal.'"

Mayor Rudy Giuliani was the American delegation's featured speaker at the July 13 conference: I was here a year and a half ago; this wasn't here. And of course, all of this is possible because of the leadership of Madame Maryam Rajavi, a truly exceptional leader.

But she also emphasized the current circumstances that spell the end of the line for the regime and called on the world to realize that the most appropriate and strategic response is found in the Resistance units forming inside Iran to expand the uprising that has already placed the regime at an impasse. She noted that the regime is incapable of reform and will not fall on its own, but that the MEK and its resistance units can and will overthrow it. She outlined the NCRI as the viable alternative to replace the regime and emphasized her movement's determination to bring about a new day and a bright future for Iran.

Hon. Rudy Giuliani, former mayor of New York City, was the American delegation's featured speaker at the event. He told the conference that:

> "This organization has grown and grown and grown, and I feel in this room today a kind of optimism that I don't remember feeling before when we were in Paris. I feel an optimism maybe because you've done a miracle here in Ashraf... I was here a year and a half ago; this wasn't here. And of course, all of this is possible because

Senator Joseph Lieberman, former Democratic party nominee for Vice President, delivered a powerful speech during the July 13 "Free Iran" conference. He told MEK members in Ashraf 3: "You don't just represent an alternative to the Iranian mullahs; you represent the right alternative."

of the leadership of Madame Maryam Rajavi, a truly exceptional leader. Just like her husband, Massoud Rajavi, who began this movement in one very brave act. He refused to swear allegiance to the Supreme Leader Khomeini to his face."

Senator Joseph Lieberman, the 2000 Democratic party's nominee for Vice President, told the audience:

"To those who advocate appeasement, it's time to stand for the people's freedom. It's time to bring a government to Iran that is accountable to the Iranians. A government of the people, by the people, for the people.

"You don't just represent an alternative to the Iranian mullahs. You represent the right alternative." He added: "Iran is ready for a new dawn and day, you are ready, we are ready."

Former U.S. Assistant Secretary of State for Political-Military Affairs, Ambassador Lincoln Bloomfield, Jr. remarked that:

> "I've been here for three days now... We heard amazing stories of courage, of conviction, of pain, of separation, of the choice of a lifetime. These were the actions of people who are stronger than me, who have a major part, who have a mission in life and who have made a choice, and they are dedicated to keeping that choice. Ladies and gentlemen, the obscuring curtain has been removed today. Never again should we hear the allegation of cult. It is gone forever."

Former U.S. Assistant Secretary of State for Political-Military Affairs, Ambassador Lincoln Bloomfield, Jr. was among the speakers at the "Free Iran" conference.

General (ret.) George W. Casey Jr., former Chief of Staff of the United States Army, addressed the resident of the Ashraf 3 in his closing remarks. He said:

> "What you have built here is a tribute to your courage. It's a tribute to your determination. And it's a tribute to your 168 comrades who lost their lives during

your journey here. It's through your grit and your determination you have cemented — cemented both literally and figuratively — Ashraf 3 as the global center for democratic resistance to the Iranian regime. And because of you and what you've done, change will come to Iran."

Rep. Lance Gooden (R-TX), member of the Committee on Financial Services, said in his speech that:

"I've learned a few things in my first seven months in office. The first thing I learned [regarding] Iran is one of the most respected people across the United States in your movement is Madame Rajavi... I look forward to visiting you all in Tehran someday very... Let's win this."

Rep. Lance Gooden (R-TX), Committee on Financial Services of the U.S. Congress, addressed the July 13 event.

Mrs. Hadassah Lieberman recalled her emotional experience as she walked through the Exhibition Hall the day before, saying:

"And when I walked through the museum yesterday, I saw the darkness, the numbers of destruction, and I heard the voices of those who shared their stories

Thousands of attendees, including more than 350 dignitaries from 47 countries, gathered in Ashraf 3.

from prison, from losing members of their family, their communities, and I saw the light in their eyes. Everyone had light, but the women who had light in their eyes struck me so clearly. They were so strong. Their lightness just came shining out. Their smiles, their transparency."

Three generations of Iranians were among the guests invited from the Iranian communities abroad to the "Free Iran" conference.

Taking in these speeches was an enthusiastic crowd of more than 2,000 MEK members residing at Ashraf 3 and dignitaries from around the world. Ashraf 3 residents were clearly heartened and encouraged by the many international figures who supported their cause after all the sacrifices and pain they and thousands of their compatriots had gone through over the past four decades.

Guests invited from the Iranian communities abroad to the "Free Iran" conference joined Ashraf 3 residents to celebrate the inauguration of the MEK's new residence in Albania.

An open-air musical concert followed the main event as Ashraf residents, representatives of the Iranians diaspora, Albanian neighbors, and political dignitaries from across the globe, poured out of Baharestan Hall to join Mrs. Rajavi on a short stroll down to the square on Mossadeq Avenue, where the concert stage and elaborate lighting and sound systems were set up. The Albanian Philharmonic Orchestra joined by Ashraf residents performed modern renditions of MEK theme songs to the delight of guests and Ashraf residents.

An open-air concert by the Albanian Philharmonic Orchestra followed the conference. The orchestra was joined by musicians from Ashraf 3 and performed modern renditions of MEK theme songs.

Musicians from Ashraf 3 and the Albanian Philharmonic Orchestra performed modern renditions of MEK theme songs following the conference.

First Secretary of Homeland Security, Governor Tom Ridge, also spoke to the audience of several thousand.

70

Former FBI director, Judge Louis Freeh, addressed the "Free Iran" conference in Ashraf 3 on July 13.

Former U.S. Marine Corps Commandant, General James Conway added a military perspective to the series of remarks.

Former U.S. Ambassador to Morocco and White House Middle East Adviser, Ambassador Marc Ginsburg, also addressed the July 13 conference.

Another member of the U.S. delegation, Amb. Robert Joseph, Former Undersecretary of State for Arms Control and International Security, spoke to the crowd on July 13.

72

(From left) Professor Ivan Sascha Sheehan, General James Conway, Ambassador Marc Ginsberg, and Ambassador Robert Joseph listen to Mrs. Rajavi's keynote speech, entitled "We will take back Iran."

Speakers from other countries included Honorable Stephen Harper, 22nd Prime Minister of Canada.

Bernard Kouchner, Former French Foreign Minister, also addressed the "Free Iran" conference.

Many European delegations each took their turn speaking to the gathering.

Members of the American delegation and Mrs. Rajavi listen to a speech by one of the international delegations.

More Events and Symposia

On July 14 and July 15, more events, gatherings, meetings and symposia were held covering a wide range of topics, including the 1988 massacre, the regime's human rights record, its treatment of women, the regime's designs for the Arab World, and the West's policy options.

A multinational conference featuring speakers from Europe and Canada convened on Sunday, July 14, 2019, to discuss support for the Iranian people's continued uprising and resistance to the regime. Dr. Matthew Offord, a member of the Conservative Party in the British House of Commons, moderated the conference. Many European figures spoke about the transformation of Ashraf 3 into a flourishing city and about the prospects for the rebuilding of Iran by the energetic people of Ashraf and Iran after the downfall of the mullahs.

Another conference featuring speakers from the Arab and Muslim world convened on Sunday, July 14, 2019, to underline a shared interest in supporting regime change in Iran. Speakers included several members of Parliament from Jordan, Morocco, Tunisia, and several Arab personalities.

A symposium focused on women's rights and attended by activists and dignitaries from around the world convened on Sunday, July 14, 2019, to hear the keynote speaker, Mrs. Rajavi, discuss the crucial role of women in the Iranian Resistance and in Ashraf 3, and their triumph over the misogynistic regime ruling Iran. Mrs. Rajavi paid tribute to brave Iranian women who gave their lives in the struggle for freedom against the mullahs. The transformation of women has inevitably led to the transformation of the men

Mrs. Rajavi was the keynote speaker at the symposium focused on women's rights on July 14. She discussed the crucial role of women in the Iranian Resistance and in Ashraf 3, and their triumph over the misogynistic regime ruling Iran.

Many activists and dignitaries from around the world listened as Mrs. Rajavi spoke at the women's rights symposium.

in the movement and together they continue to advance the collective goal of overthrowing the regime in Iran and establishing a pluralistic, gender equal republic.

Dr. Maria Ryan, CEO of Cottage Hospital and a women's rights activist, remarked at the women's conference that:

"Ten, 20 years, 50 years, 100 years, the history books are talking about you and the teachings of President-elect Rajavi. We look at the teachings of Gandhi, Confucius, Socrates, and Plato. In my country, I have great admiration for my forefathers — Abraham Lincoln, Thomas Jefferson, Benjamin Franklin. I put Madame Rajavi up with them."

Another symposium dedicated to discussing ways to hold regime officials accountable for the 1988 Massacre of political prisoners convened on Monday, July 15, 2019. Mrs. Rajavi attended the conference and reminded the attendees that "The consequences of impunity for the masterminds and perpetrators of the 1988 massacre has not been limited to the violation of human rights and perpetuation of torture and executions, but it has also emboldened the Iranian regime in the export of terrorism and in warmongering."

Additionally, she reiterated that: "The time has come for the United Nations to form an international fact-finding mission on the 1988 massacre, and for the world to recognize the right of the Iranian people to resist and struggle for the overthrow of the mullahs' religious dictatorship." She called for international support for the "Call for Justice" movement of the victims of the 1988 massacre.

Renowned Spanish Jurist Juan Garces, and UN human rights expert Tahar Boumedra, also spoke, as did several witnesses who lived through the 1988 ordeal of the massacre of Iranian political prisoners.

The Regime's Fear of the MEK and its Reprisals

The five-day conference at this epicenter of the Iranian Resistance laid bare the striking capabilities of the opposition: its discipline, structure, and unit cohesion; its ability to build and create a city on arid European soil; an unrelenting commitment to overthrowing the clerical regime, and the opposition's growing presence inside the country in the form of Resistance Units.

The "Resistance Units," are small teams of MEK activists scattered inside Iran, and entrusted with a responsibility to organize, direct, lead and support acts of protest and uprisings across the country. The units, formed in multiple Iranian cities, continue to spread rapidly. They have the ability to relocate quickly while preserving a far-reaching social orbit. These units also have the ability to convince people to participate in protests, lead strikes and formulate popular demands during demonstrations. They also prevent protests from being neutralized by the regime's operatives.

The regime started taking serious note of the MEK's role in Resistance Units after the December 28, 2017 national uprisings. At that time, more than 140 cities in almost all provinces rose up against the regime in an extraordinary show of popular force within a short span of time. These efforts demonstrated a high degree of organization and coordination. The regime's authorities quickly pointed the finger at the most organized opposition, the MEK.

> The five-day conference at this epicenter of the Iranian Resistance laid bare the striking capabilities of the opposition: its discipline, structure, and unit cohesion; its ability to build and create a city on arid European soil; an unrelenting commitment to overthrowing the clerical regime, and the opposition's growing presence inside the country in the form of Resistance Units.

80

In a speech days after the protests broke out, the regime's highest authority, Supreme Leader Ali Khamenei, acknowledged the MEK's leadership role and said, based on the most credible intelligence, "The MEK had prepared for this [protest] months ago... The MEK's media outlets had called for it."[3] Khamenei's admission was striking. A week before, the Iranian president, Hassan Rouhani, complained about the MEK's presence in France during a phone call with his French counterpart, Emmanuel Macron.[4] According to Agence France Presse (AFP), Rouhani "asked Macron to take action against a Paris-based Iranian opposition group called the Mujahedeen-e-Khalq, which he accused of fomenting the recent protests."[5]

During the 2018 uprisings, an official of the Islamic Revolutionary Guard Corps (IRGC), now on the U.S. list of

---

[3] Khamenei's website, January 9, 2018. <http://english.khamenei.ir/news/5394/Recent-damage-inflicted-on-Iran-by-U-S-will-gain-a-response>

[4] AFP, January 2, 2018. <https://en.radiofarda.com/a/iran-protests-macron-rouhani/28951795.html>

[5] U.S. Europe condemns 'unacceptable' loss of life in Iranian protests. Radio Free Europe, Radio Liberty, January 2, 2018. < https://www.rferl.org/a/iran-protests-death-toll-rises-arrests-rohani-/28950819.html>

terrorist organizations, said: "As an expert, I say the grouplet of Monafeqin (the regime's disparaging term to describe the MEK) and essentially the issue of *hypocrisy* is not dying or disappearing; Anyone who says that the hypocrites are dead is either wrong or ignorant; wrong in the sense that if he is not the enemy himself and does not have animosity with the Islamic Republic system, he is an accessory, and ignorant in the sense that he is simply unaware."[6]

The same official called it unfortunate that the regime's supporters are not aware that 90 percent of the strikes and current calls to action are the work of the counterrevolutionaries. On May 18, 2018, in the wake of major protests in the southern city of Kazeroun, the Governor of Fars Province admitted: "The MEK are playing a role in the events of Kazeroun."[7]

Video clips disseminated online and broadcast on state-run TV warned regime officials and supporters of the MEK's Resistance Units. One, published in August 2018, said: "With the support of Maryam Rajavi and the activation of the silent operatives of the MEK inside the country, multi-member 'Resistance Units' were formed inside the country and began subversive activities. In the turmoil of January 2018, the group [MEK] identified the opportunities and capacities inside the country and formally ordered operations to be launched through Resistance Units."

Members of the regime's parliament decried the MEK's "call for demonstrations," vowing "We stand against them until the last drop of our blood."[8] Friday prayer leaders, important broadcasters of the Supreme Leader's policies, joined the fray. "We want all the students of the seminaries, when there is a protest by the people, to take part in them and shout the slogans. Do not allow

6 Reza Hosseini, the advisor of the headquarters of Armed Forces Cyber Warfare. Fars News Agency (affiliated to the IRGC), August 1, 2018.
7 Iran's heightened fears of MEK dissidents are a sign of changing times. International Policy Digest, 12 Dec 2018. <https://intpolicydigest.org/2018/12/12/iran-s-heightened-fears-of-mek-dissidents-are-a-sign-of-changing-times/>
8 Hassan Nowroozi, member of Majlis (parliament), during the impeachment of Ali Rabei, Minister of Labor and Social Welfare. August 8, 2018.

the MEK to change those slogans and seize the rallies," said one during Qom's Friday prayers session.[9]

State-run newspapers even ran articles and editorials about the MEK. *Vatan-e Emrooz* daily wrote:

> "More than 70 percent of the clips calling for protest and turmoil are from channels connected to MEK. Massoud Rajavi has sent five messages about these riots since December, which is unsurpassed in recent years. The members of the organization have divided the cities among themselves, and in a multi-year process, they have organized the elite and ordinary protesters in Telegram groups. For example, in a small town there are more than 5,000 members in different groups that announce the times and places of demonstrations and coordinate them."[10]

Another newspaper wrote that "'Resistance Units' are MEK supporters inside Iran, who engage in sabotage operations at night under the name of 'Resistance units' and during the day they go to flood-stricken areas among the people under the name of 'people's councils' to help the victims."[11] A news outlet believed to be associated with Iran's intelligence sounded alarm bells that the MEK has "both the desire to overthrow" and "the capability to translate this desire into reality," adding that "this is something

> A news outlet believed to be associated with Iran's intelligence sounded alarm bells that the MEK has "both the desire to overthrow" and "the capability to translate this desire into reality,"

---

[9] Friday Prayer Imam in Pardisan district of Qom. Fars News Agency, August 5, 2018.
[10] Vatan Emrooz- State-run daily, July 3, 2018.
[11] State-run "Qabusnameh" website, May 4, 2019.

that His Excellency the Leader [Ali Khamenei] has reiterated time and again. Therefore, it is necessary that we identify them to people without any concern, to raise awareness and to prepare all the insiders against this real and serious opponent."[12]

The State-run *Tehran Press* news agency said on September 11, 2018: "It should be noted that on the Internet, especially Telegram, the enemy and especially the [MEK], have gained complete control... The culture of regime change is gaining complete control in social media networks today. If not 100%, a very significant percentage of the context is influenced by regime change culture used specifically by the MEK..."[13]

On April 19, 2019, Mahmoud Alavi, the clerical regime's Minister of Intelligence said: "Over the past year, 116 teams related to MEK have been dealt with [arrested]."[14] And, an Iranian intelligence official in northwest Iran followed the same line by saying: "Last year the MEK exploited the economic and social problems to expand its activities. Some 60 individuals associated with the group were arrested and 50 more people identified and warned."[15]

In May 2019, the MEK released a statement concerning the arrests of eleven people for supporting the organization following the regime's crackdown on protests and political dissent within the country. On April 23, the MEK released a list of 28 additional people who were arrested prior to that date on similar charges.

That same month, in May 2019, the regime sentenced MEK activist Abdullah Ghassempour, 34 years old, to death for "assembly and collusion against the regime," and "membership, propaganda and cooperation with the MEK."[16]

83

12 State-run Baharestaneh website, September 16, 2018.
13 Regime insiders express fear over the MEK's rising online popularity, May 8, 2019. <https://mek-iran.com/tag/social-media-in-iran/>
14 Radio Farda, April 20, 2019. <https://en.radiofarda.com/a/iran-s-intelligence-minister-boasts-of-wide-ranging-successes/29892972.html>
15 Ministry of Intelligence and Security (MOIS) Director General for East Azerbaijan Province, April 22, 2019.
16 MEK activist sentenced to death, Fars News Agency, May 19, 2019.

The same court sentenced three other prisoners, Mohammad Hossein Ghassempour (Abdullah's brother), Alireza Habibian (Ghassempour's relative), and Akbar Dalir to five and a half years in prison on similar charges. On May 1, 2019, the regime killed Mohammad Kord Zanganeh, another MEK activist, as he was writing anti-regime slogans on the walls of the city of Ahvaz.

In July 2019, at the time of the Ashraf 3 international conference, the Ministry of Intelligence and Security (MOIS) summoned and arrested scores of relatives and supporters of the MEK. A number of those arrested were former political prisoners who had served time in the 1980s and 1990s. The Iranian Resistance called on the UN High Commissioner for Human Rights, other relevant UN human rights officials, as well as international human rights' activists to condemn the wave of arrests in Iran.

Two weeks later, the Iranian regime's Judiciary Chief and a former Justice Minister, Mostafa Pour Mohammadi, openly defended the extrajudicial executions of thousands of MEK members in 1988. "They destroy your image all around the world. There has not been a single case of such destruction in the past 40 years, other than those in which the MEK have had the leading role. We have not yet settled the score with the MEK."[17]

Amnesty International went so far as to issue a statement condemning Pour Mohammadi's remarks: "These comments, coupled with the appointment, in March 2019, of Ebrahim Raisi, who, like Mostafa Pour Mohammadi, was involved with the mass extrajudicial executions of 1988, to the position of the head of the judiciary put survivors, family members of those executed and human rights defenders at increased risk of harassment and persecution simply for seeking truth and justice."[18]

---

17 Top Iran official defends 1988 massacre, vows to exterminate the MEK, July 30, 2019. <https://www.ncr-iran.org/en/news/human-rights/26530-top-iran-official-defends-1988-massacre-vows-to-exterminate-the-mek>
18 Iran: Shocking statements by senior official highlight impunity for 1988 prison massacres. Amnesty International Public Statement, Jul 30, 2019. <https://www.amnesty.org/download/Documents/MDE1308152019ENGLISH.pdf>

By August 2019, however, the major state-run daily *Kayhan*, known to be the mouthpiece of Supreme Leader Ali Khamenei, admitted in a stinging editorial: "The MEK has infiltrated our houses and has a huge impact on the youth."[19]

19 Iranian state-run Kayhan daily, August 9, 2019.

The Strengths of the Iranian Resistance

The MEK has what American military commanders in our delegation described as "unit cohesion." They have a structured and disciplined approach to the struggle for achieving democracy and freedom in Iran, which is essential to any liberation movement. They have an ideal, a proven methodology, and are ready to pay the price for it. This key attribute is missing from other Iranian opposition movements.

Additionally, the construction of a vast and sprawling complex in Albania demonstrates the MEK's organizational prowess. That they have built halls, facilities, infrastructure, parks, recreation centers, libraries, and clinics is also a sign of intellectual prowess insofar as they relied on their own architects to do so. In a statement signed by American Dignitaries to the July 13, 2019 gathering at Ashraf III in Albania, 34 senior former U.S. officials, military leaders, and prominent individuals observed that:

> "Ashraf III is evidence of what can be created in Iran. At the original Ashraf, the residents built a city out of the Iraqi desert. Now at Ashraf III, the residents have built a modern city in the Albanian hills. This quality of life will become available to all citizens in Iran, once the religious extremists in Tehran have been removed from power."[20]

Another remarkable strength, made noteworthy by the systemic persecution of women in contemporary Iran, is the fact that among the four generation of activists operating within the MEK,

[20] Appendix I, "Year of the Ashraf Resident," Statement by U.S. Dignitaries, July 13, 2019.

Mrs. Rajavi greets the distinguished guests attending the July 13 "Free Iran" conference in Ashraf 3.

the most prominent of these activists are women. The MEK is today headed by women, with its female cadre progressively learning and growing to lead one of the most complex political organizations in the Middle East. Many are undoubtedly inspired Mrs. Rajavi — an inspirational leader known for promoting women's rights,

"Ashraf III is evidence of what can be created in Iran. At the original Ashraf, the residents built a city out of the Iraqi desert. Now at Ashraf III, the residents have built a modern city in the Albanian hills. This quality of life will become available to all citizens in Iran, once the religious extremists in Tehran have been removed from power."

not simply in words but in actions — but also notable is the very visible way that MEK men and women support one another in carrying out their leadership responsibilities and working together to ensure maximum success.

The American delegation visiting Ashraf 3 in Albania in July 2019 was repeatedly impressed by the vitality and wisdom of the women in the MEK. Many of us spoke privately with these brave women. One prominent member of the American delegation said afterwards that this was an "illuminating experience." Their selflessness was a product of a painful history but also a love for democracy. Many had chosen to forego children and families to participate in the struggle against a tyrannical regime responsible for the suppression of the basic freedoms and human rights of more than 80 million. Others who had left families behind said they were sad to see their own children cry but accepted it to prevent the crying of millions of children in future generations, something that was heartbreaking and painful for them but at the same time a source of their strength and resolve.

We too were heartbroken when we saw images of the suffering of Iranian women in prisons. Some of them were tortured in front of their children by the regime. We heard personal stories of women whose fathers, aunts and uncles were brutally killed after being tortured by the regime, simply because they believed in the MEK's political platform of a pluralistic and democratic, secular republic. A 32-year old recounted the story of the martyrdom of his mother. Others described painful deaths and torture of their relatives. Still others explained how the Iranian regime's proxies in Iraq killed his sister and brother. We discovered that the regime was especially aggressive and hostile toward female political activists. Many of them were put in solitary confinement. When this failed to break their spirits, they were confined in small spaces for months at a time.

There was a noticeably strong bond between the military officers among us who had served at Ashraf, Iraq and with the residents now at Ashraf 3. These officers were impressed with what had been accomplished at Ashraf 3, though none were surprised. From years

The delegation of retired American military officers who had served at Ashraf in Iraq to protect its residents, emphasized how impressed they were with what has been accomplished at Ashraf 3. Behind General George Casey at the podium are (from left), col. Wesley Martin, Gen. James Conway, Brig. Gen. David Phillips, and Lt. Col. Leo McCloskey.

90

of experience they were well aware of what the residents continually accomplish and would have been surprised at anything less.

International dignitaries visit the Exhibition Hall showcasing the horrors of Iran's prisons and the savagery committed toward political prisoners.

Conclusions & Policy Recommendations

The Iranian regime has committed crimes against humanity, particularly during the 1988 massacre of thousands of political prisoners. In August 2016, for the first time, an audio recording from nearly three decades ago recalled the 1988 massacre. In it, in an extraordinarily blunt manner, Ayatollah Hossein-Ali Montazeri, then-proposed successor to the Supreme Leader, is heard telling regime judicial officials: "In my view, the biggest crime in the Islamic Republic, for which history will condemn us, has been committed at your hands, and they'll write your names as criminals in history."

These remarks are notable because Montazeri was the second highest official of the regime in 1988. When the tape came out, Mostafa Pourmohamamdi, one of the officials responsible for the murders, said that on the contrary he was "proud" of executing the MEK. He also said the regime "had not settled the score with the MEK." Amnesty International has called the massacre an example of "crimes against humanity." It has been described by human rights experts such as Geoffrey Robertson QC as one of the worst political massacres since World War II.

The massacre did not happen by accident. The regime was forced to carry it out because so many thousands of MEK supporters refused to let go of their political identity. Aware of their ultimate fate, they refused to condemn the MEK. Instead, they chanted slogans in support of the organization and its leaders. At Ashraf 3 in Albania, thousands of their images adorn walls and posters. They hail from all provinces of Iran and hundreds of cities and thousands of neighborhoods. They show the everlasting and pervasive presence of the MEK in Iranian society. These are the martyrs that have a wide surviving social network that to this day support the MEK from within Iran through intelligence and finances. The "Units of Rebellion" or "Resistance Units" that the regime fears are to a great extent supported and funded by these survivors and families. They lead anti-regime protests and rallies because they know the regime's crimes and they know that the ultimate solution is to overthrow it. They are both motivated and spirited in their quest.

In pursuit of their democratic rights and freedoms, the Iranian people have waged a remarkable resistance for freedom. Thanks to this unyielding struggle, a real, democratic, and viable alternative has emerged to the Iranian regime in the form of the MEK. No other organization has the organizational prowess, the leadership, the political platform, the social network, or the capability to stand up to the regime. The MEK is the bridge to Iran's brighter future.

The MEK espouses a Western-leaning democratic platform, has an impressive track record of resistance, and enjoys considerable support within Iran to implement that platform. Its platform calls for a democratic, free and secular Iran that is devoid of nuclear weapons. Mrs. Maryam Rajavi's Ten-point plan also calls for gender equality, respect for ethnic and minority rights, an end to Sharia law, peaceful relations with regional powers, a market economy, and other Jeffersonian ideals that Americans could be proud to support.

Tehran is justifiably frightened of the MEK, with its officials defending massacres against them and consistently warning about their role in organizing popular protests. In December 2017, when major protests broke out in the northeastern city of Mashhad and quickly spread to more than 140 cities, two narratives took shape: One said the protests were spontaneous; the other said the regime would be able to completely suppress the uprising, leading to a prolonged period (several years) of inactivity. The MEK knew that neither narrative was correct, and today they believe that there is great potential for the continuation of the country-wide anti-government uprising. Nevertheless, they are all too familiar with the obstacles that diminish the impact of protests.

In pursuit of their democratic rights and freedoms, the Iranian people have waged a remarkable resistance for freedom. Thanks to this unyielding struggle, a real, democratic, and viable alternative has emerged to the Iranian regime in the form of the MEK. No other organization has the organizational prowess, the leadership, the political platform, the social network, or the capability to stand up to the regime. The MEK is the bridge to Iran's brighter future.

93

For an uprising to be lasting and result in credible change on the ground, protests need guidance, direction and organization. With this in mind, the MEK inside the country has created, organized, and expanded two principal organizations:

1. Resistance Units: The responsibility of the Resistance units is to organize, direct, lead and support uprisings. These units have been formed in various parts of the country and are spreading rapidly. They have the ability to relocate and move quickly, while having far-reaching social orbit. These units also have the ability to convince people to participate in protests, lead the protests and formulate popular demands during demonstrations. These units also prevent the protests from being deviated or neutralized by the regime's agents.

2. Councils of Resistance: Councils of Resistance are formed among a variety of social sectors and guilds. They are formed in schools, the Bazaar, universities and factories, among other places. They work to launch protests by various sectors, including strikes. One of the joint initiatives conducted by these

councils and the resistance units was the launch of strikes and protests at the Bazaar in late June. This marked the first time that strikes and protests were intertwined in Tehran during the rule of the mullahs. The MEK was able to combine the two acts of dissent, dealing a major blow to the regime.

Unfortunately, decades of toxic allegations against the MEK, promoted by Iranian intelligence services, have aimed to obscure basic truths and to dissuade Western policymakers from recognizing these resistance units and councils as an alternative. This has limited Western policy options, with devastating consequences for everyone involved, except the regime itself.

Western policymakers in Washington D.C. and European capitals must stop appeasing the Iranian regime. Pending legislation in the U.S. House of Representatives (H.Res.374[21]) condemning Iran's state-sponsored terrorism and expressing support for the Iranian people's desire for a democratic, secular, and non-nuclear republic of Iran is a step in the right direction. The measure, which has bipartisan support, is an indication that leaders in both parties are tiring of Tehran's malign activities, including state-sponsored terrorist attacks against U.S. citizens and officials. Nevertheless, more must be done to support the democratic aspirations of the Iranian people.

Among other actions, U.S. officials should build recognition amongst Western audiences of the myriad crimes committed by the Iranian regime. Additionally, U.S. leaders are wise to communicate that there is an alternative to Iranian theocracy. The Mujahedin-e Khalq (MEK) has the organization, leadership, platform and social backing to complete regime change within Iran without foreign boots on the ground. The West should recognize the Iranian people's desire for democratic change and support the MEK and the larger coalition represented by the National Council of Resistance of Iran (NCRI). The implementation

---

21 H.Res.374, 116th Congress, "Condemning Iranian state-sponsored terrorism and expressing support for the Iranian people's desire for a democratic, secular, and non-nuclear republic of Iran." https://www.congress.gov/bill/116th-congress/house-resolution/374

of NCRI President-elect Maryam Rajavi's Ten-point Plan in Iran will not only benefit the Iranian people but millions across the world who want to see a peaceful, prosperous, non-nuclear and democratic Iran.

The battle to liberate Iran from the radical religious dictators who control it today is a battle that not only has great significance for the people of Iran but for the cause of democracy in the region and throughout the world.

In conclusion, my visit with the Iranian resistance now living in Albania revealed the following:

1. Since 1979, the Iranian regime has carried out horrific acts of suppression against the Iranian people, in addition to its sustained support for global terrorism;

2. The regime has committed crimes against humanity, particularly during the 1988 massacre of thousands of political prisoners;

3. In pursuit of their democratic rights and freedoms, the Iranian people have engaged in a courageous struggle for freedom in Iran;

4. Thanks to this long struggle, a real, democratic, and viable alternative to the existing theocratic government has emerged in the form of the MEK and the broader NCRI coalition;

5. The MEK is well-organized, has capable leadership, espouses a Western-leaning democratic platform, has an impressive track record of resistance, and enjoys the necessary support inside Iran to implement change;

6. The regime is rightly terrified of the MEK, with its officials justifying massacres against them and repeatedly warning about their role in organizing popular protests;

7. Decades of false allegations against the MEK, many promoted by Iranian intelligence services, have aimed to harm the movement's reputation as a viable alternative to clerical rule. This has only limited Western policy options and has had devastating consequences for the people of Iran.

Afterword

By Colonel (Retired) Wesley M. Martin

When the U.S. military invaded Iraq in 2003, it encountered a situation that had never been experienced before by any military. Positioned at several bases throughout Iraq was a military organization whose sole attention was focused on a third country. The Mujahedin-e Khalq (MEK) was dedicated to removing the fundamentalist regime in Iran from power, but harbored no ill will toward the U.S.

The Iranian regime's notorious rulers had been been terrorizing its own citizens, the Middle East region, and much of the world since 1979 and the MEK had its sights set on regime change in Tehran. Being pro-western, it was relatively easy for the 3,000 member MEK to work closely with the American military forces in Iraq, which resulted in strong professional relationships that exist to this day.

Unfortunately, the MEK is probably the most lied to and lied about organization in existence. As a condition to being granted Protected Person Status under the 4th Geneva Convention, each member was required to sign a statement renouncing terrorism, even though the FBI had determined not a single member had ever been a terrorist. They were also required to consolidate into a single base, northeast of Baghdad, called Camp Ashraf. Ashraf was a beautiful base, built out of the desert of Iraq.

MEK members were granted Protected Person Status in 2004 by the U.S. Government, only to be revoked in 2009. Concurrent with this, security was turned over to the government of Iraq, which by then was a firm ally of the Iranian government. While enduring oppression, rocket attacks, and ground assaults, the MEK was moved to a second camp, a former U.S. Army base called Camp Liberty, which is now remembered by the MEK as Ashraf 2.

Suffering 168 deaths and 1,487 wounded, the MEK was eventually able to move to Albania. In July of 2019 they hosted a delegation of visitors from around the world at an international conference. All but four of the guests were surprised at how fast the MEK had built a beautiful city in the Albanian countryside. Those four people were American military officers who had served with the MEK at Camp Ashraf, Iraq. The officers had already witnessed the MEK work ethic, engineering skills, speed, and thoroughness in construction, dedication to each other, and ability to stay focused in spite of the hardships they faced. They were impressed with Ashraf 3, but not surprised.

In his outstanding book — *Iran's Resurgent Resistance* — Professor Ivan Sascha Sheehan, Executive Director of the School of Public and International Affairs at the University of Baltimore, chronicles what has been accomplished by the MEK in building their new home. Professor Sheehan, a leading foreign policy scholar, also documents what the MEK endured to get to where they are today, what they are doing to preserve their history, and their continued efforts to build a free Iran and a more peaceful Middle East.

Prior to the July 2019 event, the American delegation signed a statement titled *Year of the Ashraf Resident*. A closing comment in this statement predicts the documenting of MEK history: "When that history is written, a special chapter will be dedicated to what was endured and accomplished by the MEK residents who were in Iraq and now are in Albania." In *Iran's Resurgent Resistance*, Professor Sheehan provides us with the first installment of that history.

Colonel (Retired) Wes Martin, Former Senior Antiterrorism Officer for all Coalition Forces — Iraq and former U.S. Commander, Camp Ashraf.

Appendix

Statement by American Dignitaries to the July 13, 2019 rally at Ashraf III, Albania

"Year of the Ashraf Resident"

As members of the American team, we call on our friends and colleagues from all over the world to recognize 2019 as the "Year of the Ashraf Resident."

The members of the Mujahedin-e Khalq (MeK) residing at Camps Ashraf and Liberty in Iraq from 2009 to 2016 suffered three ground assaults, five rocket attacks, deprivation of basic life support (such as food, water, and proper sanitation), and denial of reasonable access to timely medical treatment. One hundred and sixty-eight members lost their lives and 1,487 suffered injuries. For all they endured, and for their unwavering commitment to the cause of freedom, justice and a democratic Iran, they have not only earned our admiration, but they have also earned their place in the history of Iran and the world.

Now residing in central Tirana, Albania at their new encampment, appropriately named Ashraf III, on July 13, 2019, the residents will host many of their supporters and defenders from around the world. American team members participating in the event will carry with them the message of respect from all of us.

We have worked over the years for their safe relocation and to reinstate the broken promise of "protected person status" awarded in 2004 by the United States government to every resident who then resided at Camp Ashraf.

But it was the residents who persevered despite the torment and horror inflicted on them by the Iranian and Iraqi governments. The residents demonstrated their fierce determination to survive and show the world what people dedicated to democratic principles can achieve.

These democratic principles prioritize the return of Iran to its rightful owners, its citizens. The instruments of government power have been seized by religious extremists who have subjugated the Iranian people and others across the region. These religious extremists have become the number one state sponsor of terror.

The MeK and coalition of the National Council of Resistance of Iran (NCRI) are committed, through peaceful political means, to building a viable and democratic alternative to the current regime in Iran. The foundation of this commitment is the Ten Point Plan developed by NCRI President-elect Mrs. Maryam Rajavi.

No one has worked more diligently to bring the residents out of Iraq to safety than Mrs. Rajavi. Mrs. Rajavi led the worldwide relocation effort.

The residents at these Camps also demonstrated a heroic commitment to each other. Enduring the risk of death, during rocket attacks and under rifle fire, they always helped bring their wounded to safety. This is precisely what they are now trying to do for all citizens of Iran. They know their countrymen are being subjected to imprisonment, torture, and execution from a brutal regime. The MeK and the NCRI are determined to create an environment in Iran that creates a government dedicated to bettering the lives of its people, not exploiting them.

The fundamentalist government of Iran fears the MeK and the NCRI more than any other organization in the world. The regime's days are numbered, and every day that number becomes smaller.

NCRI is not dedicated to achieving power in Iran; it is dedicated to achieving democracy in Iran for all Iranians consistent with the four freedoms articulated by U.S. President Franklin D. Roosevelt: freedom of speech, freedom of worship, freedom from want, and freedom from fear.

Despite the efforts of the Iranian government to discredit the MeK and the NCRI, the truth about the regime is emerging throughout the world. Nowhere is this more evident than the MeK having been removed from its wrongful designation on the U.S. Foreign Terrorist Organization list and being replaced by the Iranian Regime's Islamic Revolutionary Guards Corps.

Ashraf III is evidence of what can be created in Iran. At the original Ashraf, the residents built a city out of the Iraqi desert. Now at Ashraf III, the residents have built a modern city in the Albanian hills. This quality of life will become available to all citizens in Iran, once the religious extremists in Tehran have been removed from power.

Last month, in Washington D.C., many thousands of supporters of the NCRI and the MeK came together to call for regime change. This same growth in support is being witnessed throughout the United States, Canada, Europe, and especially in Iran. History is on the side of the MeK and the NCRI. When that history is written, a special chapter will be dedicated to what was endured and accomplished by the MeK residents who were in Iraq and now are in Albania.

Again, we call on our colleagues from all over the world to recognize 2019 as the "Year of the Ashraf Resident."

Amb. **J. Kenneth Blackwell** — Former U.S. Representative, United Nations Human Rights Commission

Hon. **Lincoln P. Bloomfield, Jr.** — Former Special Envoy and Asst Sec State

Colonel (Ret.) **Thomas V. Cantwell,** Former US Military Commander for Camp Ashraf

General (Ret.) **George Casey** — Former U.S. Army Chief of Staff and Commander of Multi-National Forces — Iraq

Hon. **Linda Chavez** — Former Assistant to the President for Public Liaison; Chairman of the Center for Equal Opportunity

Colonel (Ret.) **John Cirafici** — Former Defense Attaché, Algiers

Gen. (Ret.) **James Conway** — Former Commandant U.S. Marine Corps

Lt. Gen. (Ret.) **David Deptula** — Former Deputy COS for Intel, Surveillance, and Reconnaissance, U.S. Air Force

Professor **Alan Dershowitz** — Professor of Law, Harvard Law School

Hon. **Louis J. Freeh** — Former Director FBI

Hon. **Newt Gingrich** — Former Speaker of the House

Hon. **Marc Ginsberg** — Former U.S. Ambassador to Morocco

Hon. **Rudy Giuliani** — Former NYC Mayor, Presidential Candidate

Hon. **Porter Goss** — Former Director of CIA, Former Chairman of House Intel Committee

General (Ret.) **James L. Jones** — Former USMC Commandant, NATO Commander, National Security Advisor to the President

Hon. **Robert Joseph** — Former Under Secretary of State for Arms Control and International Security

Hon. **Patrick Kennedy** — Former Rhode Island Congressman

Hon. **Joseph I. Lieberman** — Former Connecticut Senator

Colonel (Ret.), U.S. Army **Wesley M. Martin** — Former Senior Antiterrorism Officer, Coalition Forces — Iraq

Lt. Col. (Ret.) **Leo McCloskey** — Former US Military Commander for Camp Ashraf

Hon. **R. Bruce McColm** — President, Institute for Democratic Strategies

Colonel (Ret.) **Gary Morsch** — Former Senior Medical Officer at Ashraf

Hon. **Michael B. Mukasey** — Former US Attorney General

Brig. Gen. (Ret) **David Phillips** — Former Ashraf Commander and former 89th M.P. Brigade Commander

Hon. **Mitchell B. Reiss** — Former Ambassador, Special Envoy to the Northern Ireland Peace Process

Hon. **Bill Richardson** — Former NM Governor, Secretary of Energy, UN Ambassador, Presidential Candidate

Hon. **Tom Ridge** — Former PA Governor, Secretary Homeland Security

Hon. **John Sano** — Former Deputy Director CIA National Clandestine Service

Professor **Ivan Sascha Sheehan**, *Ph.D.* — Executive Director School of Public and International Affairs, Univ of Baltimore

Hon. **Eugene R. Sullivan** — Retired Federal Judge

Hon. **Raymond Tanter** — Former Personal Representative of Secretary of Defense to Arms Control Negotiations

Hon. **Robert Torricelli** — Former NJ Senator

Hon. **Frances Townsend** — Former Homeland Security Advisor to the President

General (Ret.) **Charles (Chuck) Wald-** Former Deputy Commander U.S. European Command

About Iran Policy Committee

The Iran Policy Committee (IPC), established in 2005, is a non-profit, nonpartisan Washington, DC-based research institute focused on US policy toward Iran. For more than fifteen years, IPC has produced actionable research and timely analyses for US officials in the legislative and executive branches, convened briefings on urgent policy matters, made fact-finding trips, interviewed relevant persons, and prompted a closer examination of the prospect of regime change by the Iranian people.

IPC's network — which includes former senior White House, State Department, Defense Department, and Intelligence Community officials, as well as prominent scholars from think-tanks and academia — have set forth their recommendations in books, reports, and op-eds, shared their expertise on a bipartisan basis, and participated in interviews and forums around the world.

IPC remains committed to educating US officials and the public about the Iranian regime's malign activities and repressive institutions and the pro-democracy opposition seeking an end to clerical rule.

Some of the IPC publications are as follows:

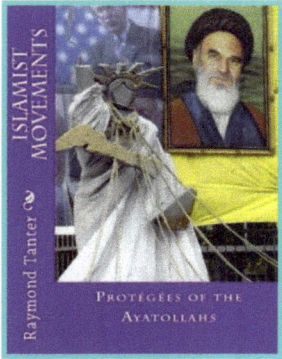

ISLAMIST MOVEMENTS

Raymond Tanter

PROTÉGÉES OF THE AYATOLLAHS

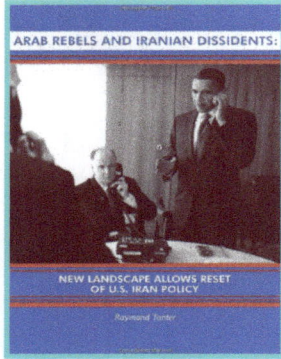

ARAB REBELS AND IRANIAN DISSIDENTS:

NEW LANDSCAPE ALLOWS RESET OF U.S. IRAN POLICY

Raymond Tanter

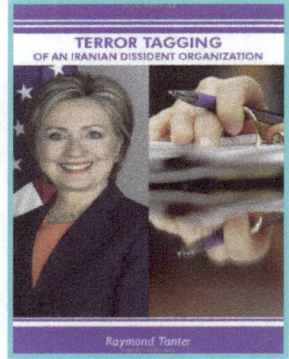

TERROR TAGGING
OF AN IRANIAN DISSIDENT ORGANIZATION

Raymond Tanter

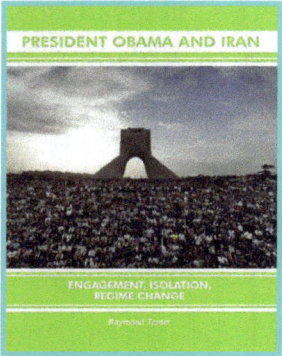

PRESIDENT OBAMA AND IRAN

ENGAGEMENT, ISOLATION, REGIME CHANGE

Raymond Tanter

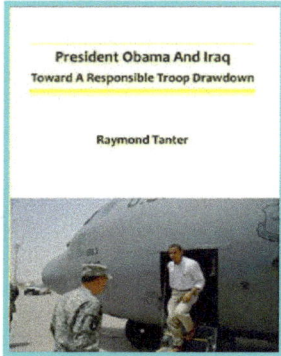

President Obama And Iraq

Toward A Responsible Troop Drawdown

Raymond Tanter

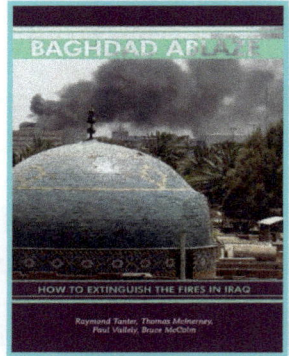

BAGHDAD ABLAZE

HOW TO EXTINGUISH THE FIRES IN IRAQ

Raymond Tanter, Thomas McInerney, Paul Vallely, Bruce McColm

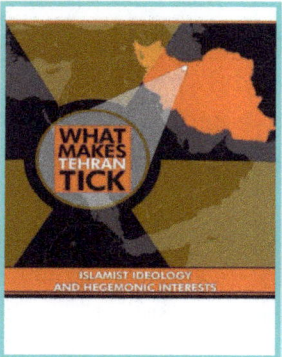

WHAT MAKES TEHRAN TICK

ISLAMIST IDEOLOGY AND HEGEMONIC INTERESTS

APPEASING THE AYATOLLAHS AND SUPPRESSING DEMOCRACY:
U.S. POLICY AND THE IRANIAN OPPOSITION

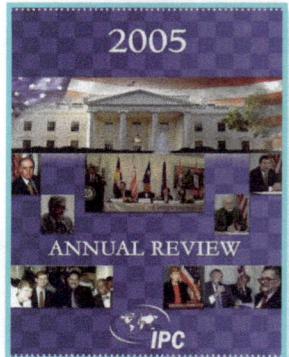

2005

ANNUAL REVIEW

IPC

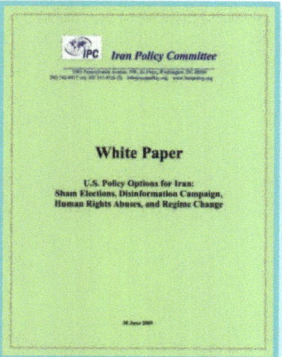

Iran Policy Committee

White Paper

U.S. Policy Options for Iran:
Sham Elections, Disinformation Campaign,
Human Rights Abuses, and Regime Change

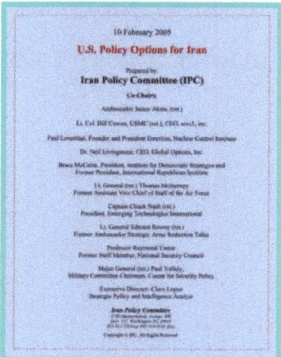

10 February 2005
U.S. Policy Options for Iran

Prepared by
Iran Policy Committee (IPC)

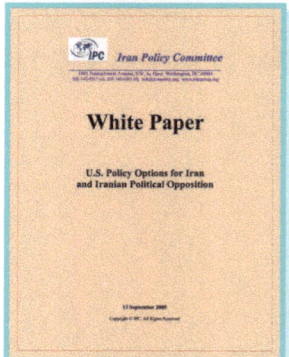

Iran Policy Committee

White Paper

U.S. Policy Options for Iran
and Iranian Political Opposition

ABOUT THE AUTHOR

Ivan Sascha Sheehan, Ph.D.

Dr. Ivan Sascha Sheehan is an Associate Professor of Public and International Affairs at the University of Baltimore where he serves as Executive Director of the School of Public and International Affairs. Dr. Sheehan's scholarship — including his first book and numerous journal articles — has involved quantitative analyses of terrorism incident data and the impact of preemptive force on terrorist activity. He has published in peer-reviewed journals on topics related to evidence-based counterterrorism policy, terrorism studies, foreign terrorist organizations, counterinsurgency, suicide terrorism, and regime change in the Middle East. The author of more than eighty publications, Dr. Sheehan's writing has appeared in *The National Interest, Foreign Policy, Fox News, Al Jazeera, The Washington Times, The Hill, Roll Call, The Washington Examiner, The Baltimore Sun, Haaretz, The Jerusalem Post, National Post, United Press International, Townhall.com, Newsmax, The Daily Caller, Independent*

Journal Review, Modern Diplomacy, International Policy Digest, New York Daily News, Citiscope, and *La Tribune.* His writing has been translated into French and Farsi and has been cited in official testimony before the Canadian parliament. Dr. Sheehan previously served as the director of the Negotiation and Conflict Management graduate program and was the founding director of the Global Affairs and Human Security graduate program in the College of Public Affairs at the University of Baltimore. An award-winning professor, Dr. Sheehan is the recipient of the 2015 University of Baltimore President's Faculty Award, the 2016 University System of Maryland Board of Regents Award, and a 2017 citation from the Maryland State Senate in recognition of "Exceptional leadership and Service to the University of Baltimore." He previously taught at the University of Massachusetts Boston, Bentley University, Tufts University, and George Mason University. Follow Dr. Sheehan at www.professorsheehan.com and @ProfSheehan.

www.ingramcontent.com/pod-product-compliance
Lightning Source LLC
Chambersburg PA
CBHW042350030426
42336CB00025B/3432